REFLECTIONS

ON THE WAY TO THE PLATFORM

AN AUTOBIOGRAPHY OF BETTY GRAY

To: Karen,
Gods Blessing
Betty Gray

PUBLISHED BY

SHINEWORTHY LIFESTYLES
A Positive Approach to Life!

www.shineworthy.com | sueann@shineworthy.com

REFLECTIONS ON THE WAY TO THE PLATFORM
AN AUTOBIOGRAPHY

ISBN-13: 978-1477410813

ISBN-10: 1477410813

SHINEWORTHY Lifestyles

Printed in the United States of America.

For information please contact: SHINEWORTHY Lifestyles, www.shineworthy.com.

DEDICATION

I dedicate this book to the Lord, my God, who is my defense, my rock, my deliverer, my strong tower, and the God who gives me a reason to live.

- Betty Gray

ACKNOWLEDGEMENT

Writing this book has been much like having and raising a baby. It started with the idea, then it became a dream, and then it became quite a chore. I often wondered how I could do such a thing.

During the process I was sometimes overwhelmed. Yet I have felt joy, excitement, wonder, and a huge sense of awe and responsibility.

For years people have encouraged me to put my stories told from the platform into a book. When God births something in you, He will make it everything He wants it to be, if we just let Him.

I am humbled that God chose a platform ministry for me. I pray this book will be everything God wants it to be.

Many people have helped birth and raise this book. I wish to thank and acknowledge:

My beloved husband and companion for 47 years, who made me believe I could do anything with God's help.

My daughter Love and her husband Bill, who promised my husband upon his deathbed to take care of me.

My Granny Martin, who had a great influence on my life.

My daughter Elvina and her family, who love me and serve the Lord.

My brothers and sisters, who love the Lord and me.

My prayer warriors, who have prayed for me each time I was on the platform.

Don and Virginia Dugan, who have been my booking agents for 30 years.

Melba Johnson, who corrected my first writings of the book.

Sue Ann Cordell, of SHINEWORTHY Lifestyles, who has encouraged me each step of the way.

Most of all, I want to thank the Lord my God who chose a little country girl to serve Him on the platform. My reflections are overwhelming of His love and plan for my life.

INTRODUCTION

"The entire world's a stage..." William Shakespeare

In the play *As You Like It*, Shakespeare compares the world to a stage, and life to a play. He catalogues the different stages in one's life. He mentions seven stages. I have chosen to add some of my own stages and to alter some of Shakespeare's stages to tell you about my life.

You are about to read about my eighty plus years, and what happened on the way to the platform. All of the stories in this book are true. They have made me who I am today. Some of the stories are humorous, and some are inspirational. As you read each one, it is my prayer that you will discover that God is, and always has been, the main player in my life.

"Delight thyself also in the LORD: and he shall give thee the desires of thine heart."

Psalm 37:4

TABLE OF CONTENTS

Shakespeare said, "All the world's a stage and all the men and women merely players. They have their exits and their entrances, and one man in his time plays many parts." Shakespeare compares it to seven stages:

PART I

I would like to add four additional stages as I write my life story,

Reflections On the Way to the Platform.

PART II

PART ONE

SETTING THE STAGE

ALL THE WORLD'S A STAGE

"...all the days ordained for me were written in your book
before one of them came to be."
Psalm 139:16 (NIV)

STAGE I

CHILD

I was born in Washington County, Indiana, and delivered by a country doctor in a farmhouse. We were poor, but I never realized it. Adequate food and much love prevailed in our home.

My parents, John and Edna Sweeney, had seven children: Loren Lee, Betty, Billy, David, Nancy, Roger, and Rena.

Loren Lee, being the oldest, always wanted to be in charge and was very responsible.

Then I came along. I, too, wanted to be in charge and found myself mothering my younger siblings most of the time.

Billy seemed to get in trouble more than the rest of us. I think it was his way of gaining attention. I remember times when he would be sitting on an old box crying because he was spanked at school, and again when he got home. One time he decided to tickle a horse from behind, and needless to say, the horse kicked him.

My brother David was very detail oriented. He was very picky about what he ate. If he loved a particular food, he wanted it all the time. He wasn't one to try new things. He loved popcorn and caramel corn. He was a fun-loving person. He passed away a few years ago.

Eight years after I was born, my sister Nancy was born. I was so happy to have a sister. I loved to play with her and to dress her. It was so nice to have another girl in the house.

Roger is much younger than me. I was grown and out of the house when he came along. When my girls were little, Uncle Roger would tease them. They remember how he would put them on top of the refrigerator. Isn't it funny what you remember from your childhood?

My youngest sibling, Rena, is my princess. I am very close to Rena. She still lives near our hometown and keeps us all informed of the happenings in the family.

When I was a little girl, I prayed most every night that God would make me a boy. I guess it was because for so many years I was the only girl in the family. One day my brothers and I were riding our bicycle. Yes, our bicycle, not bicycles. There was only one bicycle for all of us to share. My brothers knew that I wanted to be a boy, so they told me that if I would ride the bicycle down the steep hill without using the brake, I would turn into a boy. Well, I didn't turn into a boy, but I turned into a scratched and bruised mess. They took me home and told me not to tell our parents what happened. I didn't tell them, but I'm sure they figured it out. Even though I wanted to be a boy, I still wanted to be a prissy girl too.

Our family life was filled with traditions. We lived in a farmhouse, heated by a wood-burning stove. I have very fond memories of Christmas as a child. We always cut down our own Christmas tree. We decorated it with popcorn garland, construction paper chains, and silver icicles. It was the only time of year that we had candy in the house. Candied orange slices and candy canes were my favorites. We would also have peanuts in the shells for all to enjoy. At church, on the Sunday before Christmas, we would receive a treat, a brown paper bag with candy, nuts and fruit.

On Christmas morning, my father would build a fire in the stove. We had to wait until the house was warm before coming down to see what was left for us under the tree. Each child would receive one gift and a filled stocking. We always had guests join us for Christmas dinner. The guests were people who were lonely, with no place to go for the holiday. This is a tradition that I have carried on throughout my adult life.

My Granny Martin lived with us when I was a little girl (one of my Living Dramas, GRANNY, is in honor of her and the influence she had on my life). I slept with her in a featherbed. In the winter-time the covers were so heavy we couldn't even turn over. We heated an iron to put at our feet to keep them warm. Every night she read a Bible story or told me a missionary story. Then she blew out the light and we would have our prayers. The last thing she said to me at night was, "Betty Belle, God is going to use you." I never dreamed it would be on the platform.

Granny loved music, and even before my feet could reach the pedals, she taught me to chord in every key on the piano. Later, my mother provided me with piano lessons for fifty cents per lesson. A fly-swatter stayed on top of the old upright piano, and my mother used it when I added the chords to those boring beginning songs. I just couldn't help myself!

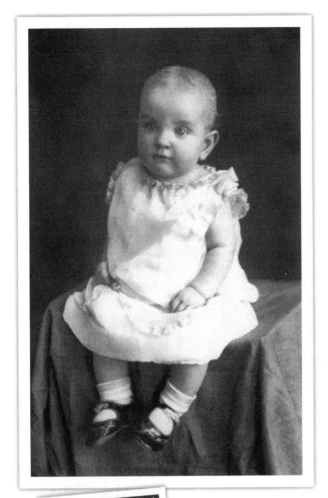

Betty Sweeney

Betty Sweeney
Four Years Old

Granny Martin

Betty Sweeney
School Girl

The Sweeney Family - 1936

SCHOOL GIRL

Prowsville Christian Church was a little country church in a farming community. It was the center of our entertainment. It was like 'the little white church in the wildwood,' that we often sing about in the church hymnals. There was no indoor plumbing, no air conditioning, and a pond that was used for all baptisms. My father was an elder, and my mother played the piano. We attended church every time the doors were opened. Revivals were held at our little church every year, and the evangelists always stayed at our home. The revivals would last 2-3 weeks at a time, and many people would come to know the Lord. I don't remember anyone coming to the Lord except at revivals. When I would get bored, I would memorize page numbers in the hymn book. To this day, I still remember that *In The Garden* is on page 15 in the hymnal that we used. During the revivals we had many great song evangelists come to our little church. They influenced my life, and at an early age I knew that's what I wanted to be when I grew up. I don't think my parents realized just how much influence the church was having on me, nor did I.

My journey to the platform began with special occasions in that little country church. On Christmas, Easter, and Mother's Day someone would ask me to recite a poem or take part in a play. Every time, my mother made sure I had a starched dress (probably made from feed-sacks) and a large matching hair ribbon. As long as I can remember, I loved being on stage.

I gave my life to the Lord at the age of eight and was baptized in a pond near the church. At that early age, my one desire was to give my entire being to my Lord and Savior, Jesus Christ.

One of my first roles in a play took place at church. My cousin was my Sunday School teacher, and she gave me the lead role in a play about the dangers of drinking alcohol. I was ten years old, and memorizing the parts came very easy for me.

One Sunday my mother became ill, which meant that at church we had no pianist. Surprisingly, my father told the minister I could play. I was thrilled to have the stage and proceeded to add some rhythm and jazz to the hymns. I thought I had done a superb job, but on the way home my father's initial words were, "If you ever jazz up a song like that in church again, I will personally come up and take you off the stage." I was crushed! I just knew I had done a fantastic job, showing off my piano skills on the platform. Maybe I was just ahead of the times. I think my musical beat was more in line with today's church music.

COUNTY SINGS

My Uncle Esten Martin was in charge of the County Sings which were held once a month at a hosting church. People came from miles around to participate in our modern day karaoke. Since my mother played the piano, she trained my older brother, Loren Lee, and me to sing duets. My uncle made sure we performed on stage at each of these County Sings.

One night on stage in the middle of a song, my brother, who was seven at the time, thought I had forgotten the right words and he put his hand over my mouth. I proceeded to bite his hand. Needless to say, a fight immediately transpired on the platform. Even at five years old I could not be upstaged on my way to the platform. My mother was mortified, to say the least, and we recognized a spanking was waiting when we arrived home. Sure enough, we got a spanking when we got home and were sent to bed. We learned our lesson and never let that happen again.

I can still remember my mother's words: "Betty Belle, does everything have to be such a production?" I did not know what that meant, but evidently I must have been quite the 'drama queen' in every situation.

Little did my mother or I realize that I was on my way to the platform.

SCHOOL DAYS

I attended grade school in a two-room building. There was one teacher for four grades. In those days, the teacher was also your friend, and sometimes she would invite the whole class to spend the night at her house. Each classroom had a double blackboard with maps that were on hooks, allowing them to be pulled down when the teacher needed them. The schoolhouse was one mile from our home. Each morning we packed our lunch bags with a sandwich, using homemade bread, and fruit. We walked the distance to school. My mother required me to wear long stockings, which I removed before I reached the school building because they were not in style. Before I reached home in the evening, I would put them back on.

My fun and carefree days of childhood included softball at recess. I could compete with any boy. I also loved to participate in school plays. I was the first to volunteer for the lead roles.

When I was thirteen, I entered a speech contest sponsored by the local 4-H Club. I was very nervous. Have you ever felt sick to your stomach because you were so nervous? Well, with fear and trembling I stepped on the stage, and my nerves began to ease up. I went on to win the local, regional, and finally the state title. Little did I know then that I was on my way to the platform.

When I entered high school, I wanted to take part in after-school activities, but without transportation I would not be able to do so. I especially wanted to take part in school productions and plays. My Grandma and Grandpa Sweeny lived in Salem, Indiana. I spent numerous nights at their home so that I could perform in school productions. I now realize what a sacrifice it was for my grandparents and my parents. It was also a sacrifice for my parents to provide the required costumes for the plays. I can still remember the play *Smiling Through* and my first formal. It was black and white. My mother purchased a used formal and altered it to fit me.

WONDER VALLEY CHRISTIAN SERVICE CAMP

Art Morris became our minister at my little country church (He later became an outstanding missionary to India). He was an energetic young college student at Cincinnati Bible College in Cincinnati, Ohio. He rode the bus to Salem, Indiana, and then walked ten miles to our home each weekend. He desired to start a Christian Service Camp, and he discovered the perfect spot only a few miles from my home. On this property were two beautiful natural waterfalls and two rundown buildings. My home church stepped out in faith and purchased this property.

The first years were exciting times. We slept on straw-ticks, created by women from the church (yes, they were full of chiggers!). Our showers were at the waterfalls (boys had one waterfall and the girls had another). Those early years provided me with wonderful spiritual and leadership training that prepared me for the platform.

At Wonder Valley, classes of chalk art and song leading were offered. Chalk art was not for me. I had no talent in that area at all. However, song leading was for me. We were taught the art of directing music, and I loved it. I loved knowing that I was leading others in worship to God, and realized that music was my passion. After just one week of training, I thought I was ready to be the world's song evangelist. My directing started in our little country church, where I convinced my father I was ready. When I think back on that time, I realize how terrible I must have been. Praise the Lord, no one told me; they just encouraged me.

It was at Wonder Valley that I dedicated my life to go wherever the Lord would send me. I observed the dedication of the workers at the camp and the joy they had in their lives, and knew they had something I wanted. I was sixteen years old when I made this decision to dedicate my life to the Lord's work. I had no idea it would be on the platform.

Betty
Age 11

Sweeney Family 1946

My Family
Bill, David, Roger, Loren Lee
Nancy, Betty, Rena
Edna and John Sweeney

Lead part in Salem High School play, 1946 (6th from left)

LOVER

As long as I can remember, I always had a boyfriend. I would kiss many a 'frog' before I found my prince.

It was at Wonder Valley Christian Camp that I was to meet my future husband, and prince, Elvin Gray. He had just returned from World War II and had seen terrible combat. He was not a camper, but in those days many of the neighboring churches would come to the camp for evening services.

Night after night I would see this dashing young man drive to camp in a new car. One night, as a camper, we were having a scavenger hunt, and my competitive spirit wanted to win. One item on the scavenger list was the longest horse hair. The camp was in the middle of nowhere in a farm community. I knew where all the barns in the area were. You were not suppose to go off the camp grounds, but when this young man drove in with his new car, I just went up to him and said, "Would you take me off the camp ground?" With a delighted look, at least I think it was, he said, "Sure." He went around to open the car door for me and I said, "Oh no, I am not suppose to go off the camp grounds, so I will need to lie down on the back seat." I told him when we were out of sight of the camp to let me know and I would show him to the closest horse barn.

I got the horse's hair, and then of course I had to lie down in the back seat as he drove back to camp. Yes, our team won!

Elvin asked me for a date and told me it was no more than fair since he had taken me off the camp ground, and if I didn't agree he would tell the camp staff. And the rest is history.

During the last evening of that week, Elvin walked forward to dedicate his life to the Lord and was to enter Cincinnati Bible Seminary that fall.

In his personal testimony, he told how he had served in the Medics during the war and saw young men curse God with their last breath. He had promised God if he could get home safely he would do everything he could to keep young people from cursing God with their last breath. This is why he had a great passion for young people.

The prayers of Elvin's mother were also answered. On the morning he left for the Army, she went into the front bedroom and knelt by the bed asking God to protect him so he would one day preach the gospel.

I had graduated from High School and was working in Salem, Indiana, at an insurance office. Elvin would drive from Cincinnati, Ohio, each weekend to see me. It was before the days of cell phones, but he called me every evening and we wrote every day. He was my Prince Charming.

On weekends Elvin preached at small country churches and wanted me on the platform to lead the music for him. Bless his heart. He couldn't carry a tune. We became a team even before we made a commitment to each other.

Elvin Gray adored me, and together we would serve the Lord. At a beautiful ceremony at Salem Christian Church, May 21, 1950, I became Mrs. Elvin Gray.

The wedding was beautiful. I wore a long white dress with a train, and a veil. The bridesmaid dresses were made by my mother and were pastel rainbow colors. I carried a bouquet of white roses. My sister Rena was the flower girl. She was at the age where little boys and girls are losing their baby teeth. She had no front teeth, and I was insistent that she kept her mouth closed for every picture. She still remembers this today, and we laugh when we talk about how hard it was for her to keep from showing her toothless smile.

My groom, being the jokester that he was, along with Ellis Wesner, the preacher who performed the ceremony, looked out over the crowd that had gathered for our wedding, and said, "Pretty good crowd, we should take up an offering."

We honeymooned in Daytona Beach, Florida. I had hardly been out of the state of Indiana so this was quite an adventure for me. We stopped at Rock City and enjoyed the scenic mountainous views on the way. I have such wonderful memories of this time in our lives. We were out to change the world together and wondered why all the preachers before us had not done so.

Elvin Gray
Soldier

Betty Sweeney and Elvin Gray
Wedding - May 21, 1950

STAGE IV

SOLDIER

SOLDIER OF THE CROSS – PREACHER'S WIFE

"Put on the full armor of God so that you can take your stand against the devil's schemes." Ephesians 6:11 (NIV)

I always loved being a preacher's wife. I never once regretted marrying Elvin. I felt it was my call to support him and lift him up. We were never discouraged at the same time. We recognized this as a gift from God. As a preacher's wife I was loved and respected. We taught our children that it was a privilege to be in the preacher's household.

I have met many preacher's wives who never liked living in a fishbowl, but never once did I wish I had married anyone but a preacher. One elderly gentleman called me 'The First Lady of the Church,' and I never took that lightly.

Our first church was in the little town of Lexington, Indiana. The church furnished a parsonage and a cat. The parsonage was a brick home that was originally a schoolhouse. There was a garden in the front yard and a maple tree that the young people loved to climb. The former preacher left the cat. His name was Tom. Tom was black and proved to be a good addition for us. I wasn't very fond of cats, but I was told that Tom was a good mouser. They were right. There would be many a time I would let the cat in the house, and I would climb on a chair while Tom captured those furry creatures.

During the week we attended Cincinnati Bible Seminary. On Friday after classes we would drive to Lexington, Indiana, for the weekends, and then on Monday morning head back to classes.

During the week in Cincinnati we stayed in a one-room apartment and shared one bathroom with four other rooms on the second floor. We ate, slept and studied in one room. It didn't matter as we were in love, and I was preparing myself for the platform with music and biblical teaching.

GO AND MAKE DISCIPLES

"Go ye therefore, and teach all nations, baptizing them in the name of the Father, and of the Son, and of the Holy Ghost." Matthew 28:19

Elvin Gray was an 'idea' person. Many times his ideas involved me on the platform. We both did many crazy things to win 'just one more' to the kingdom.

In the 1950s, revivals were an annual event in churches, and Elvin and I traveled as a team to many churches across the country leading revivals. He would preach and I would lead the song service and sing solos. Elvin thought I should have something 'extra' to use in revivals so he purchased a musical instrument called a vibraharp for me. It would be one more thing to use on the platform.

During a week long revival we would be invited to a home for lunch, and then to another home for dinner, and many times, somewhere else following the service. Every hostess wanted to outdo the other. No wonder I have a weight problem.

Loyal Harris had ministered at Elvin's home church and encouraged Elvin, as a young boy, to go into the ministry. We referred to him as Elvin's Father in the Faith. Loyal Harris ministered in the little town of Julesburg, Colorado. We were thrilled to be invited to be the guest ministers at a revival in the state of Colorado. But before the revival time arrived Brother Harris died from a heart attack. We thought the revival would be cancelled, but they still wanted us to come.

During the revival they asked us to become their ministers. My adventurous spirit said, "The Wild West, let's do it!" It was there that I found myself having to grow up quickly. The church was a divided church, and I cried myself to sleep praying many nights.

Two of our greatest blessings happened in this little town. Our two daughters, Elvina Ruth and Love Noel, were born. What a joy to be a mother. From the time both of them were born they either sat on the front pew or someone would hold them while I was on the platform.

Our girls grew up practically living at the church. They were such helpers in our ministries. I put them on the platform as soon as they could talk.

SAY AMEN DADDY, SAY AMEN

When Elvin and I first started in the ministry, we had never heard of nurseries and Junior Church. The children always sat with their parents.

Since I was on the platform, someone had to help care for my two girls. Our oldest, Elvina, with her frilly dresses, was the ideal preacher's kid. I could sit her on the front pew by the piano, and she just waited until I could sit with her.

Well, Love was quite a different story. I usually asked someone to keep her in the back of the church and feed her Cheerios until I could come off the platform and take her during the sermon. One Sunday evening when I got to her all the Cheerios were gone and she whispered to me, "I want to go home." I whispered back, "We will go home in a few minutes, now just sit still." She whispered back, "When can we go home?" I ignored her, and she said, "Mommy, when can we go home?" I said, "When Daddy says 'Amen.'" She then cupped her hands from the back of the church and yelled, "Daddy, say Amen, Daddy say Amen!"

The congregation all snickered. Her Daddy just grinned, and I took her outside and had a little laying on of the hands, which had nothing to do with religion.

LOST OFFERING PLATES

Julesburg, Colorado

I directed the choir and many times played the piano. One Sunday morning I was playing the piano. The choir was on the stage in front of me, and when it came time for the offering no one could find the offering plates.

On this particular Sunday, my husband had wanted to make a good impression as a visiting lodge had come to the services and there was standing room only. There were folding chairs down every aisle. When it came time for the offering, the elder turned to the pulpit chair and whispered, "Where are the offering plates?" Elvin looked in the podium, no offering plates. Then in a formal manner he said to one of the deacons, "Mr. Jenson, will you go to the foyer and find the offering plates, please?" Mr. Jensen returned giving a sign that he could not find them. Completely undone, Elvin said, "Mr. Jensen, will you go to the basement and find something so that we can take up the offering, please?"

I was on the piano bench and, with all of this taking a few minutes, I just simply lost it. Elvin caught my eye and gave me 'that look.' I tried to stop laughing but the tears were streaming down my face. The choir was facing me and they came unglued as well. Why is it that things are always so funny in church, when you know you should not be laughing?

By the time Mr. Jensen got back, he had large china bowls to take up the offering. When any change would hit the bowl, the clink was just too much. Elvin never cracked a smile. I was shaking in laughter.

The parsonage was a block away and after services we were walking home. I knew I was in trouble. I slipped my hand in his and said, "Wasn't that the funniest thing that you have ever seen?" For which he said, "We will never discuss that again."

Three months later Elvin's parents came from Indiana to visit us and I said, "I may get in trouble, but you have got to hear a funny story."

Elvin laughed about the lost offering plates for the first time.

TITHING

"'Bring the whole tithe into the storehouse, that there may be food in my house. Test me in this,' says the Lord Almighty, 'and see if I will not throw open the floodgates of heaven and pour out so much blessing that you will not have room enough for it.'" Malachi 3:10 (NIV)

Elvina Ruth was the first girl in the Gray family for many generations. My mother-in-law told me never to expect a girl as all the Gray family had were boys so I was not expecting a girl. Elvina would be named after her father, and Ruth from one of my favorite characters of the Bible.

She was born with an angioma tumor on her breast. The doctor said it would probably go away, but when it began to grow the doctor informed us it would have to be removed. It could not be done by radiation, as it would destroy the breast cells. It would have to be removed by plastic surgery or it would engulf her entire body.

We were making $35.00 per week, plus a parsonage, and we had no health insurance. Plastic surgery seemed impossible, but you will do anything for your children. The doctor made an appointment for us in Denver, Colorado. As we sat in the plastic surgeon's office, Elvin had very good ears and heard the surgeon tell the patient that was just before us that her surgery would be $2,000.

When it came time for our appointment, Elvin told the doctor that he would pay him for the rest of his life if he had to, but that we had to schedule the surgery.

The Sunday morning before the scheduled surgery Elvin had put his tithe in the envelope and placed it in his pocket. When the offering plate was passed, he felt the envelope and he said, "Lord, you know we need this money, but I am being faithful to your Word." With a heavy heart he placed the envelope in the offering as the plate was passed.

Elvin was ready to give the benediction and one of the elders stood up and said, "You know our little preacher and his wife are taking their daughter for surgery tomorrow. I will be standing at the back door if you would like to give them a love offering to help with the hospital expense."

There was enough money to pay the hospital and surgeon, with $26.30 left over. I gave it back to the Lord, as it was His money.

Later that same day, one of the local wheat farmers stopped by the parsonage. Elvin had been to his farm many times but he wasn't a Christian. He asked, "Where are you staying in Denver?" I told him we were going to sleep in our car and I had bought some bread and bologna for sandwiches. He pulled two hundred dollar bills out of his pocket and handed them to me. I had never seen a hundred dollar bill before that time. He said, "If this does not cover it let me know." Two hundred dollars in the 1950s was a lot of money. Not only did it pay for our hotel for the week but also for our food.

Many times Elvin shared his testimony about how he felt he would have spent his life paying off that debt had he not "brought his tithe into the storehouse and God poured out a blessing that we could not even contain" (Malachi 3:10).

BITE YOUR TONGUE, LITTLE GIRL

"But no man can tame the tongue. It is a restless evil, full of deadly poison."
James 3:8 (NIV)

The parsonage at Julesburg was one block away from the church building. The entrance to the building required a climb of ten or twelve steps.

On this Sunday evening Elvin had gone to the church to make sure everything was ready, and since I was leading the song service, I wanted to make sure I was on time.

As I got closer to the church I saw that a crowd had gathered on the steps and Elvin was standing in the center. When I got within hearing distance I saw one of the ladies of the church pointing and shaking her finger at my husband. Now, it is okay to point your finger at me, for I can defend myself, but don't you dare do that to my husband or my girls.

She was giving him 'what-to' because he had not been at a picnic that afternoon where he had been invited. Elvin was saying, "Yes, Sister. Yes, Sister, I understand Sister."

Well, I jumped in with both feet and proceeded to tell her off. I told her that the reason he was not there was because he had been called to the hospital and to please get her story straight before she attacked my husband again.

Slowly the crowd began to disperse. Mrs. Harris, who was the widow of the former preacher, took my arm and said, "Let's go to my car." I said, "I can't. I'm leading the song service." For which she said, "It can wait. Come to my car."

I thought I had done a wonderful job of putting this sister in her place, but Mrs. Harris said, "My dear, what you did in two minutes will take your husband two years to undo." I replied, "What do you mean? He was not standing up for himself." "Oh honey," she replied, "he was doing fine until you walked up."

I said, "Then what am I supposed to do?" She replied, "Just bite your tongue, little girl, and smile. It will be a silly smile, but you must control that tongue."

I saw Mrs. Harris at the North American Christian Convention a year later and after tears and hugs, she said, "How's it going, dear?" I stuck out my tongue and said, "Would you like to see my battle scars?" She frowned and did not even remember the incident until I reminded her.

DESTINATION UNKNOWN
Lawrenceburg, Indiana

Both of our parents were in failing health, and we decided we needed to find a ministry in Indiana. The Church of Christ in Lawrenceburg, Indiana, was looking for a minister and we accepted. The church in Lawrenceburg was on the Ohio River. It was a downtown church that had been covered by flood waters three times.

Young people were our love. During the ministry there, Elvin had 20 young boys paroled to him from the courts. As one of the rules, they were always to be in my Sunday School class. This Sunday School class numbered over 100 teens while we were in Lawrenceburg. Our home was always open to hundreds of youth day and night.

We started 'Destination Unknown' for teenagers on Sunday nights. They came to evening service and then a family would host the group in their home afterwards. Of course it was at an unknown destination.

Elvin made sure that our home was always open to young people to fulfill his promise to God. The promise he made as a young man was to see that they would not curse God with their last breath. I cannot begin to count the number of teens who lived with us for a period of time during their difficult teen years.

HOW DRY I AM
Lawrenceburg, Indiana

Many Sunday nights at the close of the service, there would be a baptismal service. The baptistry was in the floor of the platform. You had to move the pulpit furniture and lift up a lid to the baptistry. This was not a beautiful sight. There was a lighted cross at the front of the baptistry, so it was Elvin's idea to wait until the evening service and turn off all the lights in order to make it as impressive and meaningful as possible. During this time I was to play beautiful, soft music on the vibraharp.

On this particular evening the teenagers, waiting for 'Destination Unknown,' were sitting in their usual spot, which was the back row. They began to snicker during the baptismal service. I was giving them my evil eye, but the snickers got louder and louder.

Elvin gave the closing prayer while still standing in the baptistry, and I didn't wait until the prayer was done. I made my way down the aisle to the back of the church building to give them all a lecture. I said, "Someone just died tonight in Christian baptism and you were all laughing." One of the young men put his arm around me and said, "But Mamma Gray, did you have to play *How Dry I Am?*"

I had played *O Happy Day*, and yes, it did sound like *How Dry I Am*. I had to laugh, and I never played that hymn again for a baptismal service.

During the time in Lawrenceburg, Indiana, we were to move the congregation from the downtown location to higher ground on Ridge Avenue, away from the Ohio River. The church purchased a stately three-story mansion and used it for a few years until a new building could be erected. Many miracles took place in moving this congregation. We were truly blessed to be a part of this ministry.

The open spiral stairway led to the third floor. I remember when the organ was placed under the stairway on the first floor. One night in Vacation Bible School I was playing the organ when all of a sudden something went 'splat' on my hand. Some child had spit from the third floor, and by the time it got to me it really splattered. Some child just could not help himself.

NOW SCOOT OVER PREACHER

One of the ministries of a pastor in the 1950s was to visit the members of his congregation. My husband was making a pastoral call on one of the members who owned the local greenhouse. When he arrived at the greenhouse the owner said, "Hello, Pastor. So good to see you." While they were visiting, a customer came in. Immediately, the owner and Elvin could tell she had just a little too much to drink.

The more they talked with her, the more they realized that she would need some help getting home. The owner said, "Preacher, I think it might be a good idea if you drove her home. She can leave her car here until later."

Well, she got into the car with my husband, and he drove her home. This was a small community, and when they stopped in front of her house she said, with slurred speech, "Now, Preacher, you just scoot over, and I will take you home."

This incident brought many smiles to our lives.

OUR FIRST CALL TO FLORIDA

Love, our second child was born with bronchitis and developed problems breathing by living near the damp Ohio River. Many times I would have to take her to the local hospital and she would be given oxygen.

Elvin had two brothers, Loren and Gerald, and each year they took turns driving their Grandparents Thomas to Florida for the winter. Grandma Thomas had crippling arthritis and was in a wheelchair from the time I met her.

It was Elvin's year to drive them to Florida. He called me from Florida and said, "How would you like to move to Florida?" My reply was, "You have to have rocks in your head. No!" Then he said, "Would you at least pray about it?" For which I said, "Yes, I will pray about it." He told me that he was at a Florida ministers meeting and they were looking for someone to move to Lake Worth, Florida, to start a new church work, and he thought it was a great challenge for us.

With tongue in cheek, I did pray. I prayed, "Lord, you don't want us to move to Florida, do you?" But in the middle of the night Love woke up wheezing. I called our doctor and he met me at the hospital. Elvin was out of town and I had a sick baby. Crying, I said to the doctor, "What are we going to do with this baby?" He said, "If it were my daughter, I would move to a warmer climate away from the Ohio River." For which I said, "I don't want to move to Florida." He said, "I didn't say Florida." I knew God was calling us to Florida. We left Lawrenceburg, Indiana, and such dear friends and a thriving church for Lake Worth, Florida. There were only ten people at the new church, plus our four, and a small salary to live by faith. I thought my heart would break.

PRATT & WHITNEY COMPANY

Lake Worth, Florida

To keep bread on our table, I went to work at Pratt & Whitney Company as a secretary so that Elvin could spend full time in building a new congregation.

I did not realize what a sheltered life I had led. You can't get more sheltered than to be a little country girl from Southern Indiana, then marry a preacher. I really had no idea how the rest of the world lived, but I was to learn very soon. I was so naive, but God would provide a Christian boss who was very protective of me. For this I will always be grateful.

I was able to lead many of my co-workers to the Lord.

During that time some of the employees would give me part of their cashed pay checks so they would not lose it all on the weekends with gambling, partying and the sport Jai-Alai.

Both of our girls became an important part of our service to the Lord. They have been on the platform as long as they can remember.

Our daughter Love enjoyed having fun in church with her friends. Her Daddy had warned her many times to behave in church. One Sunday—I have no idea what she was doing now—her Daddy stopped in the middle of his sermon and asked Love to come to the elders chair and sit for the rest of the service. Oh my! He got a lecture from me behind closed doors when we got home. I guess it didn't warp her too badly. She is a preacher's wife and children's minister at the Seymour Christian Church in Seymour, Indiana. She also travels, speaking to women across the country.

FLORIDA STATE CHRISTIAN CONVENTIONS

When Elvin and I arrived in Florida there were very few Christian Churches. These churches needed fellowship, and the Florida State Christian Convention was organized.

My first time on the state convention platform, I led the song service for the convention in Jacksonville, Florida. What a thrill to be on the platform to lead hundreds of people in praise. I organized a choir of over one hundred voices from across the state to sing for the conventions.

Elvin Gray felt that since the state adult conventions were so popular that a Florida state youth convention should be started. He, along with other youth ministers from across the state, organized the Florida State Christian Youth Convention.

Thousands of young people from across the state gathered each year at a convention center. It was my honor to lead the song services from the platform at both the state adult and state youth conventions.

CENTRAL CHRISTIAN CHURCH

St. Petersburg, Florida

I have never known a minister to become a youth pastor after he had been a senior pastor. But Elvin Gray did just that. It was the height of the drug culture and he said, "I want to make sure my own girls are sheltered from the ways of the world." So he became the youth pastor at Central Christian Church in St. Petersburg, Florida.

During that time Elvin started Teen Happening, an evening once a week to invite any teenager and their friends from the church to our home. It was an informal evening of music, teaching, question time and refreshments. We began to average 120 teenagers (wall-to-wall teens). I played the piano, Jessie Allen played the organ, and the teens brought their guitars and tambourines. Our home was a 'rockin' place.' Many drug users and prostitutes came to know the Lord as a result of this program.

As the crowds began to increase at Teen Happening, Central Christian Church was generous to build on a large Florida Room to accommodate the teenagers.

We were hired as a team, Elvin as youth minister and me as minister of music. My platform was music, and I loved every moment of my time at Central Christian Church. I had over two hundred involved in the music program, consisting of a large worship choir, an orchestra, a bell choir, and special ensembles. The men's choir we named "Sons of Thunder" and the ladies' ensemble, "Joy Bells."

The desire of my heart was to see others use their talents on the stage. While at Central I wrote "King All Glorious," an Easter pageant, with a cast of over one hundred. The first year we stepped out in faith to present this production on three separate nights. The following year we added a fourth evening; the following year, a fifth evening. We gave out free tickets, and each night there was standing room only.

In the 1970s teen musicals were very popular and the senior minister, Curt Hess, gave me great freedom. I went into his office, and said, "Curt, may I bring drums in the church?" You must remember this was in the '70s and drums were a no-no. He acted as though he had not heard me and just smiled. Brother Hess told me not to ask him, and if someone complained then he could say he had not given permission. Some of the props I used for teen and children musicals must have caused him some complaints (example, building a fake fire in the baptistry to represent the fiery furnace). I am sure he got criticism, but I never knew it.

BUS MINISTRY

Elvin started a bus ministry. Bus ministries were the popular way to bring those who had no transportation to church. A fleet of buses was purchased, bringing in over two hundred children and adults each Sunday for the services. Leonard Beattie, on a voluntary basis, kept the old buses in repair and running. Leonard became my husband's lifelong friend.

The years at Central Christian are still some of my fondest memories, with lifelong friends.

BROWNSTOWN CHRISTIAN CHURCH

Brownstown, Indiana

We now had an empty nest. Elvina attended Atlanta Christian College in Atlanta, Georgia (currently known as Point University in West Point, Georgia), and Love enrolled in Cincinnati Bible College in Cincinnati, Ohio (currently known as Cincinnati University). With both girls in Bible College, Elvin's desire was to go back into the preaching ministry.

I was so happy with my musical platform, but Elvin asked me if I would begin praying about it. I did. I prayed with tongue in cheek prayers.

Elvin sent his resume to several churches. One church was excited over his resume and asked if both of us could come for an interview. The church hired him after one trial sermon and the interview. The music program at this church was terrible, and there was no room for my platform.

I cried all the way home on the flight to St. Petersburg. Elvin said, "Betty, I can stay at Central for the rest of my life; my desire is that you be happy." Whew! After all, I had to have a platform.

When Elvin said, no to this congregation, I was relieved, but I also knew I was not fulfilling the Scripture. But I needed my platform, didn't I?

When I was at Central Christian, I had many opportunities to lead the singing for conventions and large women's conferences across the country. I was invited for a national women's conference in Colorado. I always used the same format for each conference, and I had already sent the music and outline ahead for the accompanist.

On my flight to Colorado, I opened my folder to see the schedule, and to my surprise the theme of the conference was I Peter 3:1, "Wives, fit into your husband's plans" (Living Bible).

WOW, a slap in the face from the Lord! I knew this conference was for me.

When I got off the plane, I found a pay phone (before cell phones) and called my husband and I said, "Send out your resume, I am ready." He said, "Are you sure?" And I said, "Yes, and I will explain when I get home."

Brownstown Christian Church, Brownstown, Indiana, was looking for a minister. Even though it broke my heart to give up my music platform, I knew it was of the Lord. Brownstown Christian already had a choir director, Peg Lockman (who would later become my daughter Love's mother-in-law). There was not a place for my platform.

The very first Wednesday evening after we arrived, there was Bible Study followed by choir practice. I got on my knees before I left the parsonage and said, "Lord, you know I don't want to go to choir practice, but if you want me to go you will have to give me a sign."

I talked to several people following Bible Study, all excited over the new preacher's wife and open for suggestions for Daily Vacation Bible School (DVBS) and ladies groups. I breathed a sigh of relief when I heard that the choir practice had started in the sanctuary. An older lady had been waiting to speak to me, and she introduced herself and placed both hands on my hand and said, "I am waiting to take you to choir rehearsal." Okay, Lord, I just received my sign. I did join the choir that evening.

God knows the desires of your heart, and it was through the generosity of Peg Lockman who lovingly let me lead big productions—The Living Christmas Tree (Brownstown Christian Church was so generous to step out in faith and build a steel structure to hold 60 people for the Living Christmas Tree), and "King All Glorious" (Easter pageant)—which drew thousands to the church from surrounding communities and states.

When we first arrived in Jackson County, Indiana, it was late and the lights of Brownstown were shining. Elvin pulled the car over and said, "Betty, let's pray that we will have more people in attendance at Brownstown Christian Church than the population of the town." That prayer was answered with the thousands of people that would attend the productions.

I will always believe, had I not been willing to give up my musical platform, the Lord would have never opened the speaking platform.

I LOVE AMERICA MUSICAL

I was asked by the Jackson County Fair Board, Brownstown, Indiana, to direct a patriotic musical for the evening program at the grandstand for July 4, 1976, the bicentennial year.

A one-hundred-voice choir and a full orchestra were recruited from the area churches. It was an exciting evening. "I Love America" was presented before an overflowing and enthusiastic crowd in the grandstand.

Bell Choir, Fort Meyers, Florida
Betty Gray, Director (2nd row on far right)

Teen Choir
St. Petersburg, Florida

Living Christmas Tree
1981 - College Park

Teen Happening
St. Petersburg, Florida

Leading Music - 1990
State Youth Convention, Florida

Florida State
Youth Convention

SPEAKING MINISTRY BEGINS

During our ministry at Brownstown, I began to pray that the Lord would show me a new ministry. The Lord placed on my heart the need for ladies to be in the Word. With much prayer and trembling I wrote and organized ladies Bible studies. It was such a success that not only ladies of the church attended, but also ladies from the community. It was exciting to see the change in lives through the Word. The individual small groups would discuss the lesson (with questions I had written) and then gather in the sanctuary for a thirty-minute lecture that I would give on that Scripture.

At the ladies Bible studies several ladies had attended from the community, and as a result I was asked to speak at their churches for mother/daughter banquets. This would be the beginning of the speaking platform. This platform was not something I sought. I did not know "the desires of my heart" (Psalm 37:4), but God did.

I started traveling to other churches for banquets and special occasions. Elvin Gray was so generous to let me do this. He was my best encourager. People used to say to him, '"How do you handle your wife getting invited to speak when you are never asked?" He would reply, "Oh, I just love to wind her up and watch her go."

When the speaking platform was expanding to other cities and states, we had to have a heart-to-heart talk and decide if this was going to hinder the ministry at the local church. Elvin had two requests: (1) Always be home on Saturday night, and be with him on Sunday. (2) Never tell him I was tired.

Many times I would get home at 3:00 a.m. on Sunday morning and yes, I was tired, but a Sunday afternoon nap was always a must. I now see my son-in-law, Bill Lockman, following Elvin's example by letting his wife Love speak around the country. Thanks Bill, I know it is not easy.

So began the speaking platform. Many ladies come to me and say, "I want to do what you are doing," and my reply is always, "Just remain faithful in what you are doing, and God will grant the desires of your heart."

When I first started speaking, I thought people wanted to think that the speaker had it all together. I soon learned that was not what ministered to hearts, and I started sharing my weaknesses and my heartaches. After sharing my heart, ladies would line up to talk to me and share their hearts too. I have spent many long hours counseling ladies following a message.

I have learned that ladies need to laugh. Some of the true and crazy stories I told from the platform are included in this book.

One of the most humbling things from the platform is to know you have been chosen by God to hold forth His Word. Many times I experience an overwhelming feeling, and then I remember His promise, "My Word will not return unto me void" (Isaiah 55:11).

When the speaking ministry was opened to me, I met the dynamic Dixie Stuller. Dixie was a talented musician, song leader, speaker, humorist, and ventriloquist. In 1985, Dixie invited me to speak for a ladies retreat, and we became instant friends. She was an idea person. She started ladies Get-Away Weekends at various cities around the country. This was held at a choice hotel where ladies would be pampered for an entire weekend.

From the time you entered the hotel parking lot, she made sure you felt special. Your car was parked, you were given a royal welcome, and you could have your hair styled, a manicure, a pedicure, and a massage, or just take a nap.

The elegant noon luncheons included a fashion show. Ladies were asked to bring dress-up clothes for this event. The luncheon closed with singing, sharing, and a message from God's word.

The evening was set aside for spiritual nourishment. Dixie asked me to join her for each of these Get-Away Weekends across the country. At the end of the year a Caribbean cruise was also offered. These events touched hundreds of lives.

Dixie left us all too soon. What a loss to us, and a gain for heaven.

Lake Jawes, Christian Assembly
Betty Gray, Main Speaker

Leading Music - 1981

Ladies Day Speaker - 1986
Platte Valley Bible College

NACC - 1986
Betty Gray with Dixie Stutton

Great Lakes
1993

Ladies Retreat - 1996
Dayton Beach, Florida

JUSTICE

(GOD'S PLAN)

SUFFERING IS A GIFT

"If indeed we share in his sufferings in order that we may also share in his glory."
Romans 8:17b (NIV)

The Word has always sustained me in the difficult valleys of my life. People ask me how I am able to keep the faith during such times. I always reply, "By staying in the Word."

One difficult time for me was when my husband was asked to resign from the ministry. Any preacher's wife who has experienced a time like this will tell you how hurtful this can be. While he had his final meeting with the elders from this church, I decided to go to a Bible study about twenty miles away. I had heard such great reports of this large church and how the congregation flew a teacher in each week for the study. I had never been to this church, but with Bible and notebook in hand I went to the Bible study.

Satan didn't want me at that study that evening and I got lost. When I finally found the church, it was packed and there was standing room only. The lesson was on the book of Romans, chapter eight. It was wonderful teaching, and I began to take notes in shorthand of everything the speaker said so I could relate them to my husband.

On my way home, I was just rejoicing about the teaching I had heard—teachings like "If we suffer with Him we shall also reign with Him." What personal encouragement I received from His Word that night!

When I reached home, Elvin was sitting in his chair waiting for me. Without letting him say a word (I know that may be surprising) I began telling him about the teaching and how God had given this to me. I was going on and on and on. He finally said, "Betty, stop and let me tell you about my meeting." I stopped long enough for him to tell me that the elders told him we had to have both of our offices and his library cleaned out of the church within the next twenty-four hours. Now I have never been one to take such news calmly. I could not believe what I was hearing! I began to say, "Well, did you say this? Why didn't you say this? Who said that? Who do they think they are?"

For at least five minutes I was yelling and saying, "Well, I'm just going to call so and so, and give him a piece of my mind."

Finally Elvin said, "Betty, I know you are more elegant of speech than I, but right now, I don't need you to tell me what I should have done. I just need you to listen and pray with me."

For the next hour we talked and prayed. We went to bed and immediately I began to 'stew' over the situation. I was wide-eyed, and very angry. I finally slipped out of bed and went to my 'Gilgal.' Gilgal is where Joshua always went to pray after each battle. I sat in my chair and began to weep before the Lord. Then I remembered the notes from the Bible study. I took the notebook and read a story the teacher had told. When I heard the story earlier in the evening, it really did not mean that much to me.

Here is the story. It was Christmas Eve, and a little girl was saying her prayers in great anticipation of Christmas morning. This was her prayer: "Dear God, when I get my presents tomorrow, please forgive me, I may not remember, but just know I will be thinking of you."

The teacher's point: "Suffering is a gift, and when you open this present, remember that it is a gift from God in order that we may reign with Him."

Wow! I left Gilgal and went to the bedroom and woke Elvin up to tell him, "Suffering is a gift. It is a gift from God. We have just opened a gift, and we must thank him for it that we may one day reign with him."

Footnote: I have ministered to countless numbers of God's Servants who have gone through heartaches in the ministry. I include this story so you may know that any suffering you are going through is a gift that you may one day reign with Him.

ENCOURAGE ME MINISTRIES IS BORN

"'For I know the plans I have for you,' declares the LORD, 'plans to prosper you and not to harm you, plans to give you hope and a future.'" Jeremiah 29:11 (NIV)

"You intended to harm me, but God intended it for good to accomplish what is now being done, the saving of many lives." Genesis 50:20 (NIV)

When we were asked to resign from the ministry it was very difficult. This was a very deep valley for us. Elvin was the senior minister, and I was the minister of music. We were receiving two excellent salaries from this ministry. Overnight, our source of income was cut off.

We owned a beautiful three-bedroom home with a swimming pool. Even though I had been speaking for ladies retreats on weekends, we knew it was not enough income to cover our monthly expenses.

We both spent the night in tears and in prayer. The next morning Elvin said, "I'm going to go get the mail." While he was gone, I could see that feeling sorry for myself was not doing any good. I walked over to the dining room table where I had just finished writing ladies Bible study lessons on the book of Genesis. All my Bibles, commentaries, and study material were still on the table because I was preparing to write some lessons on the book of Exodus.

As I sat myself in front of the open Bible, it was open to the last chapter of Genesis—Genesis 50:20— where Joseph revealed himself to his brothers and said, *"You intended to harm me, but God intended it for good to accomplish what is now being done, the saving of many lives."*

I knew this was a direct message from the Lord. When Elvin returned, I told him God had given me this Scripture. We then knelt by the couch with both of our hands on Genesis 50:20 and told the Lord in our prayers that we did not know what this meant but that we were claiming it.

My husband, who was sixty-five at the time, sent his resume to over one hundred Christian Churches. They all wanted his experience but were not open to hiring him because of his age.

During this time in God's waiting room, even though it lasted for several weeks, God always miraculously provided. I engulfed myself in the Word and in prayer.

One morning when I was particularly discouraged, I cried out to the Lord, "Please encourage me." In just a few minutes the phone rang. It was a friend I had not heard from for many years. She had been to Florida to visit her son, and her plane had to make an emergency landing in Tampa, Florida. As they were changing planes, she said, "Tampa, Florida is where Betty Gray lives and God is telling me to call her." She told her traveling companion to tell them to hold the plane long enough for her to call me. This was before cell phones. When I answered, she gave her name and said, "Are you okay? The Lord placed you on my heart, and our plane had an emergency landing, and I just need to know if you are alright."

I knew right then that my calling out to God to encourage me had been answered. He did care.

We owned an RV, and after seeking the Lord for many weeks, we made a decision to begin a traveling ministry. After all, seeing that God had an airplane make an emergency landing at just the time I called out for encouragement, the ministry must be called *Encourage Me Ministries*. The following summer at the North American Christian Convention, we scraped together enough money to rent a booth and announce our ministry. We announced that we would be available for revivals, marriage seminars, ladies or men's retreats. We wanted to be available wherever we could be used.

Do you remember the days of mimeograph machines? We made very unprofessional flyers, but it was the only thing we could afford for the convention.

Virginia and Don Dugan had a booth close to ours. One afternoon Virginia stopped by our booth and said, "The Lord has laid on my heart the need to be your booking agent." If I remember, I laughed (hopefully not aloud), but I told her that I did not mind doing our bookings and loved office work. I thanked her anyway. When she left, Elvin said, "You were not very nice to her." I laughed and said, "Who is going to need a booking agent?" To which he replied, "She said the Lord laid it on her heart, so I think you need to consider what she said." So humbling myself, I went to her booth. I told her that I had been reprimanded by my husband, and yes, if the Lord placed this on her heart, we would love for her and her husband to be our booking agents.

That was thirty plus years ago. What God's silent servants, Don and Virginia Dugan, have done, I could never have done without them.

HAPPIEST DAYS OF OUR LIVES

Elvin drove the RV down the highway and stated, "These are the happiest days of my life. I don't have a church board to answer to, I don't have a budget, and I am serving the Lord." On long drives we memorized God's Word together.

In the summer months we parked the RV at Christian Service Camps, church parking lots, or family yards until the next engagement. In the winter months, we made sure we had Florida engagements. Yes, we were Snowbirds. It's funny to think we used to complain about those Snowbirds when we lived in Florida.

God continued to open doors for the ministry. Each year we traveled thousands of miles. We thanked Him every day for His protection.

The early years we lived completely by faith. There were many times when we did not know the source of our next meal or gas money, but God always sent someone to meet that need. There were the unexpected visitors and letters that we knew were a direct answer to prayer. Years before, I said I 'lived by faith,' but having to rely on Him completely helped me realize I really did not know the true meaning of that phrase, but I do now. Here is one example of the letters we received.

Dear Betty,

I remember the day I came to see you too. In fact I remember getting my 'marching orders' (LOL) from our Leader. The amount was equal to two of our house payments at the time ~ per His instructions to help you with 'your shelter and needs'. I must have looked a sight to you both when I pulled up in that phone company van loaded with parts and tools to work on the switching and carrier equipment and dressed in that really unattractive uniform. It makes me chuckle just thinking about it. That long driveway was kind of intimidating when I wasn't really certain that I was at the right place and was hoping you would understand what might have looked like rash behavior was simply an obedient action.

You've always had a special place in my heart as I, most likely just like many others, always felt like God led Peg to ask me to come and sing with her choir and led you to minister in Brownstown so that you could be instrumental in saving my life. After the first person that I'd asked for help told me I was lying, it was most difficult to re-summon the courage to reach out again (four years later). I will always be grateful to God and through Him to you for your non-judgmental and compassionate help. My mother is coping with Lewy Body Dementia right now and every once in a while she even mentions her thankfulness to God for your being in Brownstown and having wisdom from Him. She can remember verbatim the words you used when you spoke with her and those you used when you prayed with her for strength, wisdom, and courage.

I must go and pack for a trip to Houston and San Diego. Thanks for the stroll down memory lane. May God bless you and continue to give you His perfect words as you write to relate how His hand has guided your life and blessed so many others through your obedient service and ministry.

Ephesians 1:16, I have not stopped giving thanks for you, remembering you in my prayers. (daily)

In His love, Lisa

DRAMA MINISTRY BEGINS

In our traveling ministry Elvin kept saying, "We just need something different. You can sing, you can play the instruments, you can speak, and I can preach, but we just need something that no one else is doing." He called it a 'mouse-trap.' This became our prayer, "God, show us a new 'mouse-trap.'"

I was in Ft. Lauderdale, Florida, and a dear friend invited me to a theatre to see a one-woman dramatization. I remember at the time thinking how boring it would be for one woman to give an hour program. That evening the dramatization was about the life of Maria von Trapp from the "Sound of Music." During this dramatization I was completely mesmerized and the Holy Spirit came over me. I knew this was the mouse-trap. When I arrived back at the RV, I told Elvin I had found the mouse-trap. I explained to him that I was going to research great women of faith and present their story in a one-woman dramatization.

I began to study the life of Fanny Crosby, the blind hymn writer who wrote over eight thousand hymns. I researched her life from books at the library. Then I started writing her life story in a script as if I were Fanny. I had to keep the story within forty to forty-five minutes. Each morning, I would ride my bicycle and recite Fanny over and over and over.

Elvin and I were in a revival in Michigan, and my husband asked the minister if I could have the Thursday night service of the revival. The minister asked, "What is she going to do?" Elvin replied, "Just trust me." Mark McGiverly, the minister, trusted Elvin, and on Thursday night I presented FANNY CROSBY for the first time. I had purchased dark glasses, a long skirt, a white blouse, and had someone help me on stage as if I were really blind.

Many prayers were uttered for this first performance. With fear and trembling, I presented FANNY. The minister and congregation were ecstatic. They asked me to come back the following year to do a drama, and my reply was "Oh, you better wait a few years before I present it again." The minister replied, "No, I mean get another drama." He had no idea how many hundreds of hours it had taken me to create the first, and what I thought would be the only drama I would present.

Guthrie Veech, who is currently the President of St. Louis Christian College, was ministering in Anderson, Indiana, during my early years of dramatization. He was a great encouragement to me. He held a drama fest at the church where he ministered. Each evening Gaither Music would provide a time of music, and then I would give a drama. At that time I only had five dramas, and Guthrie wanted me to return again to do another Drama Fest. Traveling ministry was our main source of income, and because it took so many hours to research and write the scripts, I told him I just did not have the time and would not be able to do it again. He came up with an idea that would enable us to have time off the road to study, pray, create new dramas, and memorize them. He sent a letter to churches asking them to donate $20 each year. With this encouragement and the generosity of so many, I have been able to take the month of August to create a new drama each year for the past thirty years.

PRESENTS

These are some of the more than 30 Living Dramas Betty created. The descriptions are from her brochure which was created by Virginia Dugan, the booking agent for *Encourage Me Ministries*.

FANNY JANE CROSBY

Aunt Fanny, as everyone called her, was a happy spirit in spite of her blindness. Her sightless eyes make her determined to see everyone she met with Jesus' eyes. She wrote some 8000 hymns, many of which are some of the old time favorites, such as *Blessed Assurance*, to *God Be the Glory*, and *Jesus, Keep Me Near the Cross*. We know her as the mother of congregational singing, "The Queen of Gospel Hymns."

In this drama, Fanny looks back over her long life, sharing some of the stories behind her hymns, and singing them for you. She demonstrates her lively sense of humor that kept her faith vibrant in the midst of hardship.

THEME: *Complete trust in our Heavenly Father, acceptance of hardships, and seeing life from God's perspective.*

GRACIA BURNHAM

In 2001, Gracia and Martin Burnham were missionaries to the Philippines, when they were taken captive by Islamic terrorists and held for 376 days. In the rescue, Martin was killed and Gracia was wounded. This drama dramatically portrays the heroic survival and the lessons learned in those 376 days.

GOMER

In the book of Hosea, God tells his prophet Hosea to marry a prostitute! After her marriage to Hosea, she returns to her former life of prostitution. When no one wants her, she is sold on the slave market, and God asks Hosea to go buy her back and bring her home.

MARY, THE MOTHER OF JESUS

Mary, young, frightened, and alone. This is how Mary, the mother of Jesus, remembers those days after the angel's visit.

She will recount for you the day her first-born Son is taken and crucified. When Jesus cries out from the cross, "My God, my God, why hast thou forsaken me?"; Mary too cries out to her heavenly father, "My God, my God, why hast thou forsaken me?"

You will be moved by this recounting of Mary, mother of Jesus, and how she must have felt.

THEME: *Obedience and trust, divine intervention in your life.*

BATHSHEBA

"Grace that is greater than all our sins."

How would you describe Bathsheba? "Adulteress, seducer, the one that caused the mighty King David to sin?" This description would be true, but Bathsheba is willing to bare her soul before you so that you might add one more word to describe her – grace.

Can you imagine the heartache that she suffered to see her husband Uriah killed and her child dying, all because of one moment of sin? Yet, in God's wonderful grace she becomes the mother of King Solomon.

THEME: *No matter what we have done in our past we can be forgiven through His wonderful, marvelous, grace.*

GRANNY

This is a heartwarming, humorous, and touching drama of everyone's Granny! One moment you will be laughing and the next moment you will be crying.

Betty begins this drama with her famous true Grandma stories of her own grandsons, as well as other true Grandma stories she has heard across the country.

The second part of this drama is the recounting of her own maternal Granny, who taught her the deep spiritual truths.

Betty uses the autoharp to accompany herself in singing some of the hymns her Granny taught her.

DALE EVANS

Dale Evans' life story is one of great inspiration! Although she was Hollywood's Queen of the West and a household name, her life was filled with many heartaches. Her first child was born with Down Syndrome and two more children died tragically. You will be moved and touched by the faith of this woman.

IRENA SENDLER

A woman who saved 2500 Jewish children from the Warsaw Ghetto during WWII. Irena Sendler used any means possible to bring children out of the ghetto and find them safe shelter, putting her own life in danger.

DARLENE DIEBLER

"I will never leave you nor forsake you"

This is a moving and unbelievable missionary story of one woman's incredible faith in a Japanese prison camp during World War II.

"I will never leave you nor forsake you" was the Scripture that sustained her during those years of horrific torture and the loss of her husband. You will thrill at the "banana story" that saved her life.

This is a life changing and challenging story for all ages.

THEME: *No matter your hardships in life, "God will never leave you nor forsake you."*

CORRIE TEN BOOM,
A MODERN-DAY DISCIPLE

Corrie Ten Boom is a legend in our time. Corrie, along with her family, was imprisoned for the crime of hiding Jewish refugees in their home in Holland during World War II. This is the story of a woman who suffered in the Nazi concentration camps and lost everything, including her aged father and beloved sister, Betsy.

If you have ever been unjustly treated or have wondered how God could ever "work all things for your good" out of your circumstances, then this drama is for you. This touching inspirational Living Drama will thrill you.

THEME: *God takes the darkest of circumstances and turns them into good for his Kingdom.*

QUEEN ESTHER

Have you ever wondered why you were placed here upon this earth? Have you ever felt that God could not possibly take your circumstances and make anything good from them? Then Queen Esther is for you.

A young Jewish girl became the queen of the most powerful nation in the known world, and was placed there "For such a time as this." To save her Jewish people from all being murdered. She risked her own life to do what she felt God wanted her to do.

You are not here by chance. God has a plan for your life.

THEME: *You were placed here for a specific purpose.*

RUTH

Ruth is a beautiful story of how God has a plan for our lives. Ruth was a young widow willing to give up her homeland, her family and her people to follow her mother-in-law to a country that was not her own.

God took her willing heart and made it into a heart for Him. She was to find a new life and new love, which she had never dreamed would be possible, and eventually became in the bloodline of Jesus Christ.

THEME: *God's sovereign plan for your life.*

RAHAB
THE GOD OF SECOND CHANCE

Rahab is a touching story of a woman who had a second chance! She was a prostitute and yet when she found the Lord, she is mentioned in the New Testament in the bloodline of Jesus Christ.

So many people think that they can never be forgiven of their past...and this drama portrays the wonderful grace of God. We truly have a God of a Second Chance.

You will be touched by this exciting story of a woman who risked everything to have that second chance.

THEME: *God's Marvelous Grace. God can use anyone, regardless of their past.*

JOCHEBED, THE MOTHER OF MOSES

Can you imagine how Jochebed, the mother of Moses, must have felt when she placed her tiny infant son, Moses, in the bulrushes in the Nile River? This drama, "Baskets of Blessings," is fresh and unique, straight from the heart of a mother. This teaches obedience to all daughters and complete trust in God to every mother.

THEME: *Obedience of children – complete trust as a Mother.*

BETSY ROSS

This is the story of the woman who was asked by General George Washington to design a flag for the newly formed nation. Betsy was a woman who knew what it was to give up a loved one for her country, having lost three husbands in wars.

This is the story of how our country was founded on Biblical principles. Our Founding Fathers did not think you could even be called an American if you were not a Christian. This drama will stir your patriotic blood.

FUNNY STORIES FROM THE

DRAMA MINISTRY

MARY, THE MOTHER OF JESUS

Once in Oklahoma I was presenting MARY, THE MOTHER OF JESUS. The stage was already set, and someone was singing a solo in preparation for the drama. When she finished I was to enter from the back of the church auditorium, singing the song I created as *Mary's Song*. While I was waiting in the foyer I was drinking a Diet Coke. A little extra caffeine never hurts! About that time, a four year old comes out of the auditorium to use the rest room. I am in costume, and when he sees me, he just stops and stares. I said, "I am Jesus' mother." He goes on to the rest room, and when he returns to his mother he says, "Did you know Jesus' Mother drinks Diet Coke?" I am glad she did not tell me until after the program.

RAHAB, THE PROSTITUTE

Many times when I arrive at the airport I do not know the person that will be greeting me. Since people can no longer come to the gate to meet you, they go to the holding area and wait for the incoming passengers. They will often hold a sign with the name of the passenger on it. I remember one time when I flew into Greensboro, North Carolina. I was looking for a sign with my name on it, but instead I saw a strange sight. It was a large sign that read, LOOKING FOR RAHAB THE PROSTITUTE. Two gentlemen were holding up this sign. If you did not know anything about the Bible story, you would not have the slightest idea who Rahab the Prostitute would be. I usually think pretty well on my feet, but this time I didn't know what to do. So I just walked over to the sign. The gentlemen holding the sign were the minister and an elder from the host church, and they thought it was hilarious. People were watching this gray-haired lady walk to the sign, and they began nudging each other. I, of course, had to follow them down to the luggage pick-up, and the same people were still staring at me. By this time I had my faculties back and said to the preacher, "I think I will cup my hands around my mouth and say, 'Please take a number,'" but I didn't.

TWO SHOES FOR THE SAME FOOT

I had been invited to Julesburg, Colorado, where we had ministered many, many years before. They had secured the high school auditorium for me to present dramas each evening. The first drama was to be CORRIE TEN BOOM. I had packed the shoes for the dramas, and when I went to put them on I realized I had packed two shoes that were different colors, and for the same foot. Needless to say, that was the quickest drama that had ever been given, as I was in pain.

MUSICAL INSTRUMENTS

COWBELLS

These hand made musical instruments have been a great blessing to me, and to countless others around the world. In the early 1960s, we were working to build a new church in Lake Worth, Florida. That year, for the first time, I was invited to do a workshop at the national North American Christian Convention. I was thrilled and honored. The assigned topic was "Innovative Ways to Teach Children Music." I wanted to collect all the information I could for this workshop. I read in the local Lake Worth newspaper about a "Kiddies Rally" where a woman from a local church was using musical instruments to teach children. I called the church office and asked if I could meet with this lady. The secretary suggested that I attend the Kiddies Rally and then meet with the leader following the service. This sounded like a great idea, so I attended that evening. She used many novel musical instruments—the musical saw, lead crystal goblets and musical cowbells. All of the instruments greatly intrigued me. After the service, the lady graciously let me play the instruments. She accompanied me on the piano while I played each novel instrument. Then she played the instruments and I accompanied her on the piano. I was very thankful to my Granny Martin for teaching me how to play music by ear.

I was having so much fun and lost track of time. I looked at my watch and realized it was after midnight. I knew Elvin would be worried. When I arrived home he said, "Well, I hope you gathered lots of useful ideas for your workshop." I replied, "No, I don't have any ideas for my workshop, but it is going to cost you, I must have a set of cowbells."

Arnold Westphal of Michigan City, Indiana, hand made cowbells, and I ordered my first set from him. I purchased two octaves with only F sharp and B flat, which limited me in the songs I could play. I recorded accompaniment music on the piano to play along with the bells. Thus began the infamous cowbells that I played at retreats and churches before I spoke or performed a drama.

I took my first set of cowbells on a mission trip to Jamaica. It took me weeks to perfect a new song, but the native children could play it in just a few minutes. The missionary asked if I would leave the set, and I told her I would with one stipulation. If Mr. Westphal was still alive and able to make me another set, then I would leave the set for the children.

It turns out Mr. Westphal was indeed able to make another set of cowbells for me. When I received my second set, it was with two and a half octaves and included all the sharps and flats. This is the set I still use today. In the beginning, I took very good care of them and wrapped each one individually; now they just get thrown in their case. I've learned you can't hurt them.

Mr. Westphal made several sets of cowbells for others who heard me perform. He has now gone on to his reward, and I am positive he is playing the Golden Bells in heaven.

COWBELLS BRING BACK THE MUSIC

My cousin, Mary Ann Johnson, was a great musician. She loved and taught music. She and her husband Lee tragically lost a son in a car accident. Mary Ann was driving the car and her life was also in balance for many days. After healing from the injuries, the Johnsons had another child, a little girl they named Beth. Sadly, when Beth was just a few years old, she was diagnosed with Reyes syndrome. Hundreds of people across the nation were praying. I just knew God could not take a second child from this godly family. Then one day, I received word of Beth's death. I was devastated. At that time I was living in Florida, and each summer my family went home to Indiana to visit our parents. I knew I had to go see Mary Ann, but what do you say to someone who has lost two children?

I had just received my cowbells, and knowing how much she loved music, I took the bells with me when I went to visit with her. She said to me, "Music has left me." I had already carried in the case with the bells and told her that I would just leave them with her while we were in Indiana and would pick them up before we returned to Florida.

In her testimony later, she told how the cowbells brought music back into her life. Later, she ordered a set of cowbells of her own. I must say she was so much better than I, but we had so much fun when we played cowbell duets. I took the lead and she played the harmony part. Yes, she really was much better than me on the cowbells.

STORIES FROM COWBELLS

I have had embarrassing situations with the cowbells. One night at a church in Jacksonville, Florida, the table with the bells was sitting close to the platform steps. I hit one of the larger bells and knocked it off the table. It went rolling down the platform steps with a clang. Elvin was sitting on the front row. He picked it up and rang it while I was in the middle of my song; then he brought it back to the table. He got much louder applause than I did.

MINISTERS' WIVES RETREAT

Many years ago at the Indiana State Ministers' Wives Retreat, I was in charge of the music on Friday night and had used the cowbells, which were always a good icebreaker. On Saturday, someone else was in charge of the music, and I was the featured speaker. On Saturday morning, several ministers' wives requested that I play the cowbells. I told them I would be happy to do so, but they would have to ask the lady in charge, especially the person leading the music that morning.

The lady in charge of the retreat then came to me and said, "Just before you speak, why don't you play your cowbells?" I told her I would be happy to do so. I must also tell you that it was April 1st (April Fool's Day). Some minister's wife had scotch-taped every clapper to the bell. Everyone was in on the joke but me and that is why they wanted me to play. I know you think your minister's wife is an angel. Well, not necessarily! I never did find out who was responsible.

COWBELLS AT MINISTERS RETREAT

Not only are ministers' wives devious, so are the ministers. I was playing the cowbells for a minister's retreat, and some minister came and rearranged each bell. They have to be set up on a chromatic scale. I always play with recorded music. I gave the nod to the person in charge of the sound equipment and began to play. It sounded terrible because every bell was out of place. I asked the sound engineer to stop the accompaniment while I put the bells back in place. I never did find out who did it, but to this day, before I begin playing, I make sure I check the bells to see if they are in the proper order.

AND ALL THE PEOPLE SAID, "MOO"

Danny Spainhour had been a youth minister when we were in Tampa, Florida. He moved to North Carolina and invited me to give a drama for a Sunday evening service at his church. His mother's name was Betty. Danny and I had been very close and he called me "Mamma Betty #2."

As I often do, I played the Musical Cowbells before I dressed for the drama. As I was leaving the platform, the people were applauding and Danny said, "Everyone said...?" I was expecting the congregation to say, "Amen." Instead, he had made a huge placard that said, "MOO." About five hundred people mooed me off the platform.

When I got home I told my husband about the incident, and he said, "I have heard of people being booed, but never mooed off the stage."

WHY THEY ARE CALLED COWBELLS

When I was growing up on the farm, my father put a cowbell on what he called the 'lead cow.' This allowed us to locate the cows in the evening to bring them to the barn for milking. I grew up knowing the function of a cowbell. Since many children no longer grow up on a farm or know the reason they are called cowbells, I always try to explain to them why they are called cowbells.

Following an engagement where I had explained earlier why they are called cowbells, a young man came up to me and said, "Mrs. Gray, that is not why they put cowbells on the cow's neck." Well, I knew it was, but my mother also taught me to be kind, so I didn't argue the point. He said, "The reason they put the bell on the cow's neck is because their horns won't work." I didn't see that one coming!

THE GIFT OF THE LEAD CRYSTAL GOBLETS

One of my speaking events was at the ladies retreat at Lake Region Christian Assembly in Crown Point, Indiana. I spoke on Friday evening, and just before I spoke for the Saturday morning session, I played the cowbells again. I had chosen the old hymn *Whispering Hope* since the words went with my message on "Hope." But while I was playing this old hymn, a lady in a blue dress ran from the room. After the morning service I looked for this lady. I asked several ladies if they knew who the lady was so I could speak to her and counsel or pray with her. No one knew.

The following week I received a letter from the lady. She poured her heart out to me about how bitter and angry she was with God. Her husband had died, and she was so angry with God, she had determined she would never attend church again. Her friend had invited her to the ladies retreat. She said, "The speaker is funny, she is a musician, and you will love her." The letter went on to tell me how she had been blessed by the Friday night message, and even though she was uncomfortable, she knew what I was saying was truth. On Saturday morning when I played *Whispering Hope* (which was her deceased mother's favorite hymn), she knew how upset her mother would be that she was angry with God and had turned her back on Him. She told me that she just had to go home and get things right with the Lord. Her closing line in the letter was, "Thank you for using the cowbells to bring me back to the Lord." Needless to say, I shed a few tears.

When I reread the letter I thought, "I wonder if Mr. Westphal, who made the cowbells, is still living?" I sent a note to him and wrote, "Mr. Westphal, I am not sure if this letter will be returned as I have not heard from you for several years, but I am enclosing a letter that blessed me for playing the bells, and I want you to be blessed for making them."

A week later I received a letter in shaky handwriting which stated: "Dear Mrs. Gray, Thank you so much for sharing the letter. How it blessed me. I am dying of cancer, and want you to know that I have made over 700 sets of musical bells, and you are the first one to thank me. So, I would like to give you my set of Musical Lead Crystal Goblets." He continued, "I cannot send them to you as they are too fragile to mail, but you will be placed in my will to receive the goblets. Please pick them up in Michigan City, Indiana when you are in the area."

Several months later, we were in Northern Indiana and my husband said, "You must get those Musical Goblets." I was really not too thrilled to receive them. The only person I had seen play the Musical Goblets had taken over an hour to place water in the goblets and then sometimes they were still not quite in tune. But with my husband's insistence, we drove to Michigan City, Indiana. It was before the days of the GPS. I went to a phone booth and found the phone number, but when I dialed the number, there was no answer. I then began calling all the Westphals in the phone book. Finally, I got an answer and asked if they knew an Arnold Westphal, to which I received a positive response. The voice replied that he had passed away several weeks ago, but that he knew the name of his son. I then called the son, and when the man answered I said, "This is Betty Gray." He said, "Oh thank the Lord, your name was in my Father's will and we had no idea who Betty Gray was."

He gave me directions to his home and I received the Lead Crystal Goblets. I said to the son, "Where is the water line on the goblets?" He replied, "Mrs. Gray, there is no water line. My father had perfect pitch and picked these goblets up from all across the world to make his personal set. It is the only set that we know of that does not require water. These are very valuable."

Mr. Westphal had screwed each goblet on a board and had made wooden cases for them. I can set them up in about five minutes.

Elvin always said, "The cowbells are country, but the goblets are Carnegie Hall." By rubbing your fingers around the rims, using vinegar to cut any grease on your hands, they sound like a violin.

Footnote: When I was on tour in Michigan I broke one of the goblets. Needless to say, I was heartsick. I now have to add water to one goblet. But only one.

ANGKLUNG BAMBOO MUSICAL INSTRUMENTS

First Christian Church in Fort Myers, Florida, built a beautiful new par-sonage for their preacher and his wife. It was the first new home I had ever lived in, and I could even pick out the colors for carpeting. I chose purple carpeting, my favorite color, with all white furniture. It was lovely. I am sure the next preacher's wife could have killed me.

Carl and Grace Fish, and children Monica and Phillip, missionaries from Indonesia, needed a place in Florida to stay while on furlough. I felt since the Lord had given me such a lovely home, I needed to share it with His Servants. It was a delightful time.

After that year, they returned to Indonesia and spent another five years on the mission field. When it was time for their next furlough, they used their suitcases to bring back an entire set of Angklung Bamboo Musical Instruments for me, in thanks for the year spent in our home.

By then we were ministering in St. Petersburg, Florida, and I organized a choir playing the Angklungs. To have an entire set of Anklung Bamboo Musical Instruments was unheard of in the musical world.

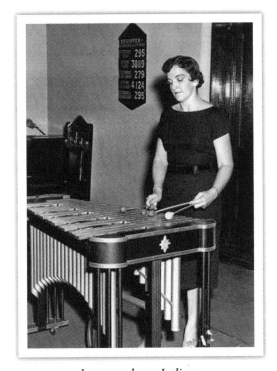

Betty Gray and Mary Ann Johnson
1975

Lawrenceburg, Indiana

Ladies Retreat
1996
Daytona, Florida

Angklung Choir - 1972

Pennsylvania - 2006

PANTALOON

Shakespeare, you have nothing on me.
I have two stories for this stage.

"A miserable heart means a miserable life; a cheerful heart fills the day with song."
Proverbs 15:15 (The Message)

MY FAMOUS PANTALOON STORY

For many years I have spent my winters in Florida where winters are wonderfully warm and sunny. I would spend about six months in Florida, leaving Indiana in October and returning in April. When I moved into a new home in Seymour, Indiana, I thought about how much fun it would be to stay in Indiana for the holidays, and then go to Florida after the first of the year. So I decided to try it. It had been a long time since I had experienced any cold weather. I was freezing!

I told my friend, Janet Breon, who lives in Pennsylvania, how cold I was and she said, "Oh Betty, you need cuddle-duds." Cuddle-duds are long underwear. She purchased a pair of black cuddle-duds for me, and I received them in the mail that very week.

I had an engagement in December in Brazil, Indiana. This was about a two-hour drive from Seymour. The snow was flying and the wind was blowing, so I decided to try out my new cuddle-duds. I got dressed and went over my check list to see if I had everything for the drama, RUTH: costume, accessories, water, contract, and the directions to the church. Once I checked everything off the list, I drove the two hours for the scheduled program. I arrived at the church in plenty of time to get a sound and light check, set up the cowbells, rehearse with the sound system, locate the dressing room, and go over the pre-check list to make sure I was ready to enter the platform at the proper time.

On the way to the dressing room, I passed a full-length mirror in the hallway, and as I caught a reflection of myself I thought, "My, these slacks have shrunk." Now in the dressing room I always have my costume and accessories all laid out so I can dress in record time. When I began to change into the costume, I realized I did not have on any slacks, only the cuddle-duds. Thank goodness my jacket had covered part of me. Keep in mind I had already been on the stage for all the pre-check. I had set up the display in the foyer, greeted people, and I only had my pantaloons on!

When I find myself in such a situation, I get the giggles and cannot quit. I had to get myself in shape to give the program on the book of RUTH. When the drama was over, the lady in charge of the day said, "Mrs. Gray, we will wait until you change costume before we begin the noon meal." To which I replied, "Oh I will just eat in my costume." I never eat in my costumes. This is a no-no as all the costumes have to be sent to the dry-cleaners; however, this time I had to make an exception.

I could not wait until the morning was over to call my daughter Love and tell her the "pantaloon story." I have used this story from the platform many times.

My son-in-law Bill Lockman says, "All people do stupid things. My wife Love and my mother-in-law Betty are the only two I know that are dumb enough to tell the world."

THE TRIAL OF THE PANTY HOSE

When we started the traveling ministry of *Encourage Me Ministries*, we made sure we had engagements in the state of Florida for the winter months.

We had parked the RV in St. Petersburg, Florida, for my first speaking engagement for the winter. Elvin and I had ministered in this community for several years and made lifelong, forever friends.

One dear sister, Vicki Baldwin, a ninety-four-year-old dear friend, had no children and through the years of our ministry in St. Petersburg she had adopted us as her children. We called her "Mamma Vicky," though we were not related. She was in a nursing home in St. Petersburg. I looked at my watch and had almost an hour before I needed to be at my engagement, so

I thought I would just stop by and tell her that we were back for the winter. Then I remembered that I always took her Hershey's Kisses candy. She was not supposed to have them, but at ninety-four I thought that she should have her wish.

I ran into the large grocery store, in a hurry of course, and they had just filled the salad bar. A piece of ice was on the floor. I slipped and fell and broke my right arm. Now I didn't know it was broken, but of course I was embarrassed. I did get the candy and told Mamma Vicky about my fall. She said, "Are you hurt?" and I said, "I don't think so. It just stings, and I was embarrassed."

By the afternoon session at the retreat, my right arm was throbbing so much I had to put it on the podium to alleviate the pain.

When I got into the car to go home, I could not turn the ignition with my right hand. Now I was certain I had a broken arm although I had never had a broken bone. When I got back to the RV, I said to my dear husband, "I think you have a problem." He said, "What is my problem?" I replied, "I think your wife has broken her arm." Now, if you have never been to a metropolitan hospital emergency room on a Friday night, you don't know what you are missing. I had to wait my turn with drunks and wounded people. Then I realized I was one of them.

When it finally came my turn, the doctor put my broken arm in a temporary cast and said I had to go to a specialist on Monday. When we came out of the room, more people had joined the group, and I thought I might as well give them something to talk about. I looked up at Elvin and said very loudly, "I told you not to hit me."

The following Friday night, I was to speak at a minister's retirement party. By this time, I had a cast from my wrist to my shoulder. Have you ever tried to wear dressy clothes when you have a cast on your arm? I had to ask my husband to help me dress for the evening. It took us a good hour to find something appropriate for the evening and something I could wear that would slip over the cast. When we did finally find something, I said, "Now you have to help me with my panty hose," to which he said, "Go without them." I told him we would be at the head table and there was no way I could go without panty hose. I know it is the style now, but it wasn't then. So I proceeded to tell him how to gather them up. At this point, he was out of patience. He said, "I have often wondered why a woman can't just step into her panty hose like a man steps into his pants." I replied, "It won't work!" You must remember I was at his mercy. He stretched those things out like a man would step into his pants, and you ladies all know what happened. I got a run in four pairs. I said, "Now, let's do it my way. This is not working." To which he stated, "I have already decided that; so you lie down on the bed and stick your legs straight up, and I will stand over you." I was laughing so hard the tears were streaming down my face, and he said, "Not funny. Hold still. How do you expect me to get these on?" He finally thought he had a good aim and came down with a swoosh! Of course my right foot went all the way through the hose. I sat up and said, "STOP! We are doing it my way! Go back to pair number four because it is the least injured, and get the fingernail polish."

All the way to the retirement party I was still snickering. He did not think there was anything to snicker about.

At the party, I just sat still at the head table. I told everyone it was my broken arm. That was not the truth. I was glued together with nail polish, and I could not move.

The next day, I went out and bought thigh-high hose to save a good marriage.

TRAVELS

"If I go up to the heavens, you are there; if I make my bed in the depths, you are there. If I rise on the wings of the dawn, if I settle on the far side of the sea, even there your hand will guide me, your right hand will hold me fast."
Psalm 139:8-10 (NIV)

When I was a little girl, it was a rare occasion for me to travel out of Washington County, and unheard of to travel out of the state of Indiana. One of my first recollections of travel was when I was eight years of age. Aunt Alice Cook treated my brother Loren Lee and me to a train ride from Salem, Indiana, to Campbellsburg, Indiana. This was a distance of 10 miles. Little did I know what God had in store for me later in life.

Psalm 139:8-9 has always meant so much to me. I have been honored and privileged to be on platforms in thirty-eight states and thirty foreign countries.

CRUISES

For our 25th wedding anniversary, it was my heart's desire to save enough money so Elvin and I could celebrate on a Caribbean cruise. For one year I saved—from my grocery money, the money Elvin received when performing wedding ceremonies, and from giving private piano lessons. The day finally arrived, and we boarded the ship for our dream vacation.

The first night on the cruise I got seasick. This was before the ships had stabilizers. I thought to myself, "This was not what I had saved all this money for." In desperation, I went to the doctor on board. He gave me a shot, and I was healed! What a wonderful time we had!

Each night we attended the ship's entertainment, but it was so ungodly that Elvin and I slipped out onto the deck and watched the moonlight. One night after the entertainment had once again become so offensive, we walked out on the deck, and I said, "What a shame. I love being waited on. I love the luxury, I love the food, and I love having my nightgown laid out for me each evening. What a shame God can't use this to His glory." Then I said, "Hey, I have an idea." When I said "I have an idea," Elvin said, "Oh no," because he knew it would mean work for him. This was thirty years ago before any of the top religious leaders had even thought of Christian cruises. But in 1980 I obtained top Christian speakers and musicians to lead our Christian cruise. I continued to do this for thirty years (with the exception of the years of Elvin's failing health).

Oh what outstanding Christian speakers and Christian artists I have had for these wonderful years. I would not begin to list them as I might omit someone. Many have now gone on to their reward; they have crossed over the waters of Jordan.

The cruises have included many Caribbean cruises, numerous Alaskan cruises, a Hawaiian cruise, Panama Canal cruise, Mexican cruise, and a European cruise. What a wonderful platform for dramas on each cruise!

FOREIGN PLATFORMS

The platforms have extended to many foreign countries. I cannot count the times I have been to mission fields in Haiti. I have always commented about Haiti being one of the poorest countries in the world. "I have never been dirtier, I have never been hungrier, I have never been hotter, but I have never been happier."

Each time when I reached my home, I placed my hand on the refrigerator, on an ice cube, on my bed, on my air conditioner, and on my pillow, and thanked God for what He has given me and for the blessing of living in this country.

Virginia Dugan, Seed Sowers Mission in Jérémie, Haiti, asked me to do dramas on the platform. I told her I could speak through an interpreter, but I would lose my train of thought on a memorized script doing a drama. She insisted. My able interpreter, Paulette Princeton stood behind me as I presented MARY, THE MOTHER OF JESUS. When I exited the platform as MARY, THE MOTHER OF JESUS, I left singing *Mary's Song*. As I was going down the aisle, the people began to mutter something in their native tongue. I said to Paulette, "Oh, I bombed, didn't I?" She said, "'No, they are asking for you to tell them more, more, and more." For the next hour, I stood and answered their questions about Jesus. It was a platform moment I will never forget.

GOODY BAGS IN HAITI

After my first trip to Haiti, I saw such a need. The things we just take for granted can be such a luxury to the Haitians. So it was my goal to collect miniature soaps, shampoos, lotions, and the like from our overnight stay in hotels. I also asked ladies, as I spoke across the country, to clean out their scarf drawer and bring me scarves they were no longer wearing. The next ladies retreat in Haiti, I wanted to put all of these things in a "Goody-Bag" for each lady. I asked the missionary for suggestions of what we might use for a "Goody-Bag" and she said, "Put them in a plastic grocery bag, because they love grocery bags with handles. I was touched because this is something we throw away. The missionary then added two Band-Aids, a spool of thread and a needle to our collection of scarves, lotions, soaps, and shampoos. How thrilled the Haitian ladies were! Some of the ladies cried and asked, "Who gave these to us?" We replied, "Your sisters in America."

Several ladies in attendance walked twenty miles one way over rough terrain. Those who had shoes carried them while they walked, so they could have shoes for the retreat. They slept on mats stretched on the ground. We are so blessed!

MARRIAGE TEACHING IN HAITI

Leon D'orleans, ministers in the poorest section of Port-au-Prince, Haiti, in a city called Cité-Soleil, which is actually located on the city garbage heap. Leon asked if I would come to Haiti and teach the women about morals and marriage. He explained to me that women who become Christians in Haiti know nothing about morals or the sanctity of marriage.

I had many notes on marriage seminars and was ready to tackle this assignment. When I got to Haiti, the information I had prepared for morals and marriage in America did not relate to these ladies.

The first night I stayed up all night asking questions of the missionary and redoing all my notes. For example, I have always loved I Peter 3:7 in the Living Bible that says your wife is the 'weaker vessel,' and my example to ladies in America is that we are the weaker vessel and we want to be treated like a china cup, not a coffee mug. This is an excellent illustration in our country, but not in Haiti. They have never seen a china cup.

I taught three times each day. At the close of each session, the ladies asked questions through the interpreter. One question was, "Ask Mrs. Gray what she would do if her unsaved husband brought home three or four women and had sex with them in front of her. If she refused to enjoy it, he would take his belt to her."

When the interpreter asked me that question, I said, "Tell her I have no idea. I cannot comprehend that." Then I continued, "But ask her to come forward and I will pray for her." As the tears flowed from her eyes and mine, the Lord placed on my heart an idea for the cheap bangle bracelet I was wearing. I slid it off my arm and on to hers and I said, "Place this bracelet, which has no beginning and no end, on your arm, and when your husband does this, you hold on to this bracelet and remember God's love for you has no beginning and no end." I added, "And I promise to tell ladies all across the country to pray for you."

I had her kneel and asked any lady who knew what she was going through to come and place their hands on her and pray with me. About thirty ladies came forward to place their hands on her. The ground was wet with all our tears. Again, a platform I will never forget.

KOREA

In the year 2000, I was invited by the United States Army to present dramas to our troops in Korea. This came through an invitation of Major Karen Diefendorf, a chaplain stationed in South Korea. She had seen one of my dramas, the story of DARLENE DIEBLER, about a missionary held captive during WWII. If she could get clearance from the United States government, she wanted to know if I would come to Korea and present this drama to our troops. I will never forget her words. "I want our troops to know if they are ever taken captive that it will be their faith and then their training that will sustain them."

What a glorious three weeks I spent in South Korea! Each day the Major had her driver pick me up in a Hummer; then she met me at the airbase, and we took a Black Hawk helicopter from base to base.

The Korean people were so generous in giving gifts. One of the customs of each Army base, in their gesture of welcoming me, was to present me with a lavish gift and their Unit's coin. This is called "coining."

I was also privileged to go to the DMZ line of North Korea. Major Diefendorf was such a wonderful hostess. She took me to many sights and shopping places in South Korea. I will never forget this platform!

HOW DO I GET INTO THIS BLACK HAWK?

In South Korea Major Diefendorf would meet me each day where we boarded a Black Hawk helicopter. The first day I looked at the helicopter and noticed that the entrance door was several feet off the ground. I wondered how I was going to hoist my 170-pound body into that door. As I was thinking this, one of the officers put down his hand for Major Diefendorf to step into and then lifted her into the helicopter. I knew I was next. With his muscle and a little huffing, I was in the helicopter. The next day a stool was provided for the officer and me.

WHO IS BOB HOPE?

My five grandsons thought it was totally cool that I could ride in a Hummer and in a Black Hawk helicopter. My youngest grandson Stevie asked, "Now Ba (his nick-name for me), what are you going to do in Korea?" I told him, "Just call me Bob Hope, since I am going to entertain the troops." He replied, "Who is Bob Hope?" You have to love the generation differences!

AUSTRALIA/NEW ZEALAND

Julie Nevel is a dear friend of mine from Pennsylvania. She is also a recording artist. She and I traveled 'down under' to Australia/New Zealand where we shared the platform by encouraging our sister churches and missionaries.

In Australia/New Zealand, they drive on the 'wrong side' of the road, and their 'round-a-bouts' are confusing. We both had obtained our International Driver's License. Julie asked, "Do you want to drive?" I said, "You drive and I will pray."

One of my dreams has always been to see the Opera House in Sydney, Australia. The missionaries were so generous to let me fulfill that dream. I stood on the platform of the world-famous Opera House. Please note, I just stood.

The kangaroos and koala bears are real, not just something on a postcard. The platforms in Australia/New Zealand are a lifelong memory for me.

ISRAEL

My first trip to Israel was with Curt and Joan Hess. He ministered at Central Christian Church in St. Petersburg, Florida, at the time. My mother had been very ill, and I received a call to come immediately to Indiana one week before our scheduled trip. My mother passed away, and the memorial service was two days before the scheduled trip. Of course we cancelled our lifelong dream of going to the Holy Land.

After the service, Curt insisted that we meet them in New York, and he informed us that he had not given our tickets to anyone. Would we still consider coming? I will never forget that trip. I cried the entire time. That ten-day spiritual journey was such a healing time for me.

I was bitten with the Holy Land bug. There is something about going to the Holy Land that feels like home. I have made eight trips to Israel.

GUEST OF THE ISRAELI GOVERNMENT

While I was minister of music at Westshore Christian Church in Tampa, Florida, I was invited by the Israeli government to travel on an all-expense-paid trip to Israel. Outstanding music directors from all over the United States were invited. It was the Israeli government's goal to have each director invited bring their choirs on a tour of Israel. They would arrange for our choirs to sing at various functions while in Israel. Many of the musicians were music directors from colleges and universities from across our country. Many of them could have cared less about the spiritual sights. While Joseph, our guide, explained the sites, many would be talking and not listening. When Joseph found out I was interested, he had me sit in the front seat of the bus each day. He would just talk to me and not try to talk above the others. Normally on a tour like this, one of the rules is to rotate seating on the bus each day.

At night when we were in the hotel, Joseph and I would meet for dinner, and I could ask any questions I might have about his knowledge of this land. Joseph and I would talk for hours. When I went to my room, I would weep for the men and women from the music departments of our colleges and universities who were not interested and were even making light of the things of God. They were only interested in a free trip and the finest of food and wine. This was one of the most informative, but one of the saddest tours, I have ever taken.

JUST ONE MORE NOTCH ON MY STAFF

"Thy rod and thy staff they comfort me." Psalm 23:4

On one of my tours of Israel, we were privileged to receive an invitation to have coffee in a Bedouin shepherd's tent. I was thrilled with this extra opportunity.

Our guide instructed us to sit on the floor of the tent. The floor was covered with rugs. We were told that the coffee would be very strong and bitter. We were also told that we could ask questions.

The coffee was terrible! But there were many questions asked by our group. While I was looking around this humble tent, I noticed this Bedouin shepherd had a staff. I also noticed that it had been carved about one-half the way from the bottom, and the carving was beautiful.

I asked about the carving on the staff. Here is the explanation given by the shepherd.

"When a shepherd is guarding his sheep and something happens, he does not have pen and notebook to record this; thus he makes a carving on his staff to remind him of what God has done." These Scriptures immediately came to mind.

"Then he took his staff in his hand, chose five smooth stones from the stream, put them in the pouch of his shepherd's bag and, with his sling in his hand, approached the Philistine." I Samuel 17:40 (NIV)

Hebrews 11:21 says, "By faith Jacob, when he was dying, blessed each of

Joseph's sons, and worshiped as he leaned on the top of his staff."

What a comfort to know what God has done for us in the past is just one more notch on our staff.

EUROPE

In 1972 Standard Publishing Company in Cincinnati, Ohio, asked Elvin and I to lead a group of young people from all across the country on a mission trip to encourage our missionaries in Europe. My responsibility was to organize a choir to sing on the platform at each mission point.

We could only take one suitcase and we stayed in hostels all over Europe. In many places we carried our suitcases up two or three flights of stairs, but we were young then and it didn't matter. We borrowed money so both of our girls, Elvina and Love, could go with us.

Each missionary was so generous in showing us the sights in each country.

PLATFORMS - 30 FOREIGN COUNTRIES - 38 STATES

Even though I have been on the platform of thirty foreign countries and thirty-eight states, I have always been glad to get home. I wonder if that is why, as we travel through this life, we look forward to our eternal home?

*Old Stockholm's
narrow streets -
1998*

Cruises

Israel - 1978

Teaching in Port-au-Prince, Haiti - 1993

Alaska - July 1985

Ireland - 2000
Sharyl Bledsoe and
Betty Gray

Bavaria - 1990

Interview on Christian Radio - 2004
Newcastle, Australia
Julie Nevel and Betty Gray

Major Diefendorf and Betty Gray
- Korea 2001

New Castle, Australia - 2004
Betty Gray and Julie Nevel

Australia - 2004

Betty Gray and Julie Nevel
- 2011

Ladies Retreat,
Alaska
2005

Alaska - July 2006

PART TWO

ON THE STAGE

ALL THE WORLD'S A STAGE

"'For I know the plans I have for you,' declares the Lord, 'plans to prosper you and not to harm you, plans to give you hope and a future.'"

Jeremiah 29:11 (NIV)

PERILS

"He ordered his angels to guard you wherever you go." Psalm 91:11 (The Message)

I have been hosted in some of the finest of homes. The host and hostesses have fulfilled the Scripture in giving their finest and best to me on the way to the platform. Graciously, hundreds have given beyond their means to see that I was comfortable. Many have even given up their own bed so that I could have my privacy. For all of this I can only say, "Thank you, and God's blessings."

On the way to the platform, I started speaking long before ladies retreats at campgrounds were modern or comfortable. I have endured many lumpy mattresses, smelly outdoor toilets, and numerous top bunks. I remember one campground where I slept in my clothes to keep warm, and the next morning there was no hot water for a shower.

Since I lived in the state of Florida, many times I forgot to put in enough warm clothing for campgrounds, especially in the mountains. I will never forget Janet Breon, in Pennsylvania, loaning me her beautifully handmade jacket to wear because I was freezing. I wore it for the entire retreat. At the end of the retreat, she gave me the jacket. Could it be that it was too dirty for her to want it back? Since that time, Janet has remained a lifelong, forever friend.

LOST LUGGAGE

I fly thousands of miles each year, and I always pray that my luggage will make it to my destination. I praise the Lord that, to this date, I have never lost a costume. Many times I have had to go to the platform wearing the same clothes and makeup that I had put on earlier that morning before I left my home. But never has a costume been lost. I consider that to be a miracle.

I have, however, arrived at my destination only to find that I had picked up the wrong luggage at the airport. At one engagement the minister and I had driven over two hours from the airport when his wife called to say that someone else had my luggage. Since I did have the costume luggage with me, I was able to make it to the platform in time. The minister drove back to the airport to exchange the luggage. After that night, I decided to do things differently. So if you see a wild marking on the luggage at baggage claim, it is mine.

WARDROBE MALFUNCTION

I am thankful for the invention of the safety pin! Enough said.

DRESSING ROOMS

I have changed into my costumes in many a broom closet or furnace room. Sometimes freezing cold, and other times, burning up from no air-conditioning.

LOST COWBELLS

For many years, I carried my musical cowbells on flights with me. When the rules changed and passengers were only allowed to have one carry-on, I started packing them in my suitcase. Since the man who made the bells by hand has gone to Glory, and I know they cannot be replaced, I am always fearful that they may get lost. The cowbells have only been lost one time. I was speaking at a retreat, and on the last day of the retreat the airline found the missing bells. They had someone drive over one hundred and fifty miles just to deliver the cowbells back to me. All the ladies at the retreat in North Carolina offered a prayer of thanks that day.

SHARING WITH ANIMALS

Please don't form an opinion of me when I tell you that I really am not an animal lover. Animals are just okay. They have their place and when my girls were growing up their Daddy felt they needed a pet. With two girls and a husband that was a vote of three to one, so we had pets.

When I was a guest in a home, sometimes a family pet would find its way into my room. It would jump on my bed while I was sound asleep. 'Freaking out' is putting it mildly.

MY BIRD STORY

For those of you who loves birds, I'm sorry. But I am truly not a lover of birds. When I was growing up on the farm in southern Indiana, I was spurred by a turkey, and my brother Loren had to take a stick and knock the turkey from my leg. I still have a scar from that incident. I have always said that is why I really do not like birds.

Following a ladies retreat, I was a guest in a minister's home in the state of South Carolina. When we arrived at the home, we were seated at the dining room table where the hostess served us something cold to drink. In the living room, there was a large birdcage and a huge bird. The minister said, "You don't mind if I let the bird out, do you?" My reply was "Yes, I do mind." Thinking I was just joking, he let this huge feathered friend fly around the room and just above my head. I did a nose-dive under the dining room table. My daughter Love was also a speaker for the retreat, and she and the minister were laughing hysterically. I did not think it was the least bit funny!

DIET COKE

I used to be a Diet Coke®aholic. I would always pack Diet Coke in my carry-on bag. When it got too heavy, I began packing the six-pack in my suitcase. My husband would say over and over to me, "One day that is going to explode because the storage area is not pressurized." But since I had done it many times, it was just part of my packing process. I was flying to Pennsylvania for a ladies retreat, and when I arrived and opened my suitcase, everything was wet and brown! You guessed it. The Diet Coke had exploded. I was rooming with about twenty other women, and there was no privacy and no place to hang my 'unmentionables.' I tried to wash out my clothes as best I could. Needless to say, I was not the best-dressed speaker for the ladies retreat in the Pennsylvania mountains that year.

MISSED FLIGHTS

I have missed more flights and run through more airports than O.J. Simpson. Some of you are too young to remember that advertisement. One time I missed a connecting flight and arrived just in time to be escorted onto the platform to speak. I had not eaten and was not even able to freshen up. After the service no one offered me anything to eat. I also found I was to room in the dormitory with the ladies. The only bunk left was a top bunk, and they had forgotten to bring bedding for the speaker. Some of the ladies shared their blankets. There were no sheets. I felt I should make a good impression since I was their speaker, so I opened my Bible to read before I went to sleep. I opened it up to where Paul said, "In whatever situation therewith to be content." I laughed out loud and wrote in the margin of my Bible these words, "Paul, you never have been at a ladies retreat." I closed my Bible and went to sleep.

MOTHER/DAUGHTER BANQUETS

I've been blessed to have the opportunity to speak at many mother/daughter banquets. This is where I started on the platform. Years ago this was the annual event of many churches, and to speak from babies to grandmothers was always a challenge.

My first mother/daughter banquet speech was "Mother-Goose Mothers." I felt I could keep the children entertained as well as the adults with this topic. I had the children quote the nursery rhyme and then I made a spiritual application.

Through the years I have learned to block out all the distractions of babies crying, children talking, and little girls coming on the platform while I was speaking to play with my shoes or pull on my dress.

LITTLE SLEEP

When *Encourage Me Ministries* began, many nights my husband drove all night while I slept. I can recall one night we were so exhausted, and I was to be on the platform three different times the following day, so we decided to get a motel room. This was before Interstates and only 'Mom and Pop Motels' were available in small towns. It was after midnight and my husband had to wake the owners to secure a room. Elvin had already paid cash for the room. When we got to the room it was very dirty. I pulled sheets back to see if they were clean, and I took the bathroom towels and placed them on the bed. I also had him get a blanket from the car to pull over me and then slept with my clothes on. For security, I had my husband pull the dresser over in front of our door. When we got in bed, with tongue in cheek I asked Elvin, "Do you suppose they serve breakfast with the room?" He said, "If they do, it would be goat cheese." He always had such a dry sense of humor, and I was so exhausted that I could not stop the giggles.

NO SENSE OF DIRECTION

I am so directionally challenged! Retreat Centers and Christian Campgrounds are always in the 'boonies' and I have been lost more times than I can count. When I look back on the thousands of miles I have driven, I am so thankful for a Heavenly Father, and his wise sense of direction that guided me to the platform.

I am also thankful for the modern convenience of Map Quest and my trusty GPS. The first time I used my GPS I was so amazed. I kept thanking the Lord for giving someone the knowledge to create a GPS to know exactly where I was, and then He reminded me that it wasn't such a great invention. He had known where I was since my conception.

STORIES
FROM THE PLATFORM

I'M WALKING

"Yea, though I walk through the valley of the shadow..." Psalm 23:4

As we traveled in our RV for *Encourage Me Ministries*, Virginia Dugan, our booking agent, was always so diligent to book us in the same area to save on travel expenses.

We had attended the North American Christian Convention in St. Louis, Missouri, and Virginia had us booked in several churches in the surrounding area. We parked our RV in the church parking lot where I was scheduled for a ladies banquet following the convention.

I don't remember my topic that evening, but following the program, several ladies came up to speak to me. As I was speaking, I saw a young lady crying, and I was glad to see she was waiting in the line to speak to me. Out of the corner of my eye, I noticed that each time she got close enough to speak to me, she turned and went to the end of the line. She did this about three times, so while I was still speaking to the lady in front of me, I reached over with my right hand and grabbed this young lady. She broke free from my grip and said, "I just need to be last."

When she did get to me, she put her arms around my neck and began to sob. I said, "Do you know where we can find a classroom where we can be alone?" She led me to a classroom and closed the door. Again, she fell into my arms and sobbed. I told her, "I have all night. My RV is parked out in the church parking lot. Just take your time to tell me your story."

When she finally composed herself, she said, "Mrs. Gray, you couldn't possibly know me. You spoke several years ago at St. Louis Christian College where I was a student." She continued, "You spoke on Psalm 23, and I still recall the message. You said, 'Yea, though I walk.' You said, 'Walking is a steady progression. When you are in a valley you may try to run through it. You may feel like you are lying down in the valley. But the Word says, "walk." And you will walk through it, you will not stay there.' You also said, 'Yea, though I walk through the valley of the shadow. There is never a shadow without a light up ahead.' Your closing words were, 'If you are ever in the valley of the shadow of death, and you can't pray, just say "Lord, I'm walking; Lord, I'm walking."' She continued, "To demonstrate that, you kept walking across the stage and saying, 'Lord, I'm walking; Lord I'm walking.'" She then relayed that on the way back to their dorms the young girls who had attended the presentation were mocking me, "Lord, I'm walking; Lord, I'm walking."

After more tears and a long pause, she said, "Now I must tell you my story. I married the love of my life, a student from St. Louis Christian College. He went into the ministry. We became discouraged and left the ministry. At first we were 'pew-warmers,' and then we just let other things come before the Lord. We gradually stopped going to church and would find other things to occupy our time most every Sunday."

"We had a little girl. She was the apple of our eyes. When she was two years of age, she woke up with a high fever and went into convulsions, and I rushed her to the doctor. By that time she had gone into a coma. They had to air lift us to the Children's Hospital in Kansas City, Missouri. I had not prayed or read my Bible for many months, but as I was in the deepest valley of my life, your words from many years ago came back to me, 'Lord I'm walking, Lord I'm walking.'"

"When we got to the hospital I paced up and down the hallway praying that prayer, 'Lord, I'm walking; Lord, I'm walking.'" Then through more sobs she said, "My little girl had an inoperable brain tumor and she died. But Mrs. Gray, I want you to know that my husband and I are back serving the Lord, and we just keep on walking. Thank you for being used of the Lord."

Footnote: I had forgotten about the message at St. Louis Christian College but I say to you who are reading this: If there ever comes a time in your life when you are walking that valley of the shadow and you can't pray, just say,

"Lord, I'm walking; Lord, I'm walking." He will bring you through that valley.

AN ABUSED WIFE

I was booked for five performances for a drama fest in Anderson, Indiana. This was early in my drama ministry. I had four dramas ready but was still working on one more, JOCHEBED, THE MOTHER OF MOSES. I researched, wrote and memorized my dramas, and it takes many hours of orally repeating the drama before I am ready to perform before a live audience. That week we were staying in a local motel, and I needed to go over my new drama for the evening performance. I asked my husband if he would go to the lobby and give me about one hour of rehearsal time in the motel room. He took a book and said he would be back in about an hour. Every time I rehearse a drama, I include all the expressions like I would do before an audience. The drama was set during a time when God's people were slaves in Egypt. I started JOCHEBED by shouting, "Why, Why, Why, must we live this way? Why don't you do something (pointing to people)? Why don't you do something?" And then I scream, "I can't live this way any longer!"

There was a knock on the door. I stopped long enough to go to the door and the maid rushed in the room. She said, "Are you all right?" She then frantically went into the bathroom and looked in the closets, looking for something. I was clueless as to what was going on. And she said, "Was someone beating you?" I then realized she heard me yelling and thought I was being abused. I tried to explain to her that I was fine, and that I was just rehearsing for the drama I was doing that evening. I should have told her to go to the lobby and have my husband arrested.

LEFT OVER CHICKEN-GRAVY

"Give, and it will be given to you..." Luke 6:38 (NIV)

When we ministered in Lawrenceburg, Indiana, we had a neighbor Dr. Terrill. After the death of Dr. Terrill's wife, his children felt that he no longer should do any cooking for himself and placed all his cooking utensils in the garbage can.

I was working in the yard, and I spotted Dr. Terrill going through his garbage. I walked over and asked if he had lost something. He told me his children felt that he did not need to cook, that he could eat out every meal, and they had thrown away all his cooking utensils, so he was digging them out of the garbage and returning them to the house. I said, "Dr. Terrill, do you like to cook?" He replied, "No, I don't know how to cook, but I do not want to eat all my meals at a restaurant. I like a home-cooked meal." I said, "Dr. Terrill, I cook every meal and I would be happy to share my left-overs with you." Dr. Terrill was thrilled and replied, "Mrs. Gray, I would be happy to buy the meat for your meals if you would just bring me your left-overs." On a limited preacher's salary, this was music to my ears.

That night for dinner I had fried chicken, mashed potatoes, a vegetable, and chicken gravy. When I asked Elvin to take the tray over to Dr. Terrill, he looked at the tray and he stated, "Betty, I'll take the meal over, but don't send that chicken gravy. It is cold, and it looks disgusting." I didn't think Elvin would ever know, so I placed a cloth over the tray and also sent the chicken gravy. I was such an obedient wife.

About one hour later, the doorbell rang and my husband went to the door. It was Dr. Terrill with the tray and the dishes. He said to Elvin, "Your wife is an excellent cook. If she was a few years older, I would take her away from you. What a wonderful meal, and I especially enjoyed the left-over chicken gravy." Oops, I had been caught. That night I realized that even our cold leftover chicken gravy could be a blessing to someone. How many times have I been guilty of throwing away my leftovers and missed out on being a blessing to others?

THOU GOD SEEST ME

"Thou God seest me." Genesis 16:13

Several years ago, I was flying to a retreat in Colorado. I was still study-ing for the three messages I was to give at this retreat. Since I knew I had a three-hour flight, I had my notes and my Bible in my hand when I boarded the plane.

After getting settled into my seat, the man sitting beside me said, "I see you are a Believer." I told him I certainly was and was traveling to Colorado to speak at a ladies retreat. He said, "Could I see your Bible?" I handed it to him and he replied, "May I look at the fly leaves of your Bible?" I had never had anyone ask that question, and I said, "Certainly." The things I had written in the fly leaves of my Bible interested the man. He asked me why I had written such things, and what it meant to me. We had a beautiful time sharing my thoughts and explaining why I had written such things. He then opened his briefcase and took out his Bible and handed it to me so that I could see what he had written in his Bible. One Scripture was Genesis 16:13 — "Thou God seest me." He said, "What does that Scripture mean to you?" I then shared how I felt the all-seeing eye of God was upon me at all times and quoted several Scriptures about the eye of God. He then said, "That is good, but to me that Scripture means not that God is spying on me, but that God loves me so much that He can't take His eyes off of me." I immediately wrote his words in the fly leaf of my Bible. Thank you, Lord. *"Thou God seest me."*

YOU ARE AN ORIGINAL

"I praise you because I am fearfully and wonderfully made." Psalm 139:14 (NIV)

Elvin's parents, Arthur and Alberta Gray, purchased a furnished home in Florida where they spent the winter months. As their health began to decline, they decided to sell the property. They told their three sons, my husband Elvin and his brothers Loren and Gerald, to remove any of the antique furnishings they might want. Elvin chose several items, including a beautiful old chair. The only problem was the chair's bottom had been woven cane at one time and had worn out. I told Elvin numerous times to have it repaired, but with his busy schedule the unrepaired chair remained in our family room. It was a beautiful antique chair, so I placed a needlepoint cushion over the broken seat. When a guest sat in the chair, the cushion squished and fell through the bottom.

The next time I had a garage sale, I put the chair in the garage sale and put a ten-dollar price tag on it. I would have sold it for five dollars. My husband came home for lunch, picked up the chair, and placed it back in its place in the room. Several years passed, and Elvin had not taken the chair for repair. When the next garage sale came around, I put a five-dollar price tag on it. I would have sold it for two dollars. Elvin must have remembered the chair and came home from the office, and without saying a word, he just placed it in the car trunk and took it to be repaired.

Several weeks later when he picked up the chair and brought it home, Elvin came in with one of those "I told you so" grins. I said, "Okay, how much did it cost?" He enjoyed telling me that the man who repaired the chair had offered him five hundred dollars for it. The chair was an original and had the date carved on the bottom, along with the designer's name. I still have this chair with a lovely afghan draped over it. What made this chair escalate in value from five dollars to five hundred dollars? The fact that it was an original, just like you. You are God's original design. There is no one else with your DNA or your fingerprints. He made you in His own image.

CONDITIONED TO THE DARKNESS

"But the way of the wicked is like deep darkness; they do not know what makes them stumble." Proverbs 4:19 (NIV)

The year Elvin was in charge of the Florida State Youth Convention, he wanted to invite an outstanding featured speaker. After much prayer and searching, he invited Sketch Erickson, a Christian artist, to speak. I will never forget the following story Mr. Erickson told from the platform. He told the audience that he was celebrating his twenty-fifth wedding anniversary, and he wanted to make the celebration a very special one. Someone recommended he take his wife to a restaurant where the food was excellent and violinists came and played your favorite song at each table. It would be expensive, but for a twenty-fifth anniversary it was a must.

Mr. Erickson liked the suggestion and made a reservation at this nice restaurant. When the evening arrived, they were escorted to their table. He said it was everything he had hoped for, including the dimly lit candles that established a romantic setting. When the waitress handed Mr. Erickson the menu, he had to strain to see the menu because of the dim lights. The waitress saw him straining and she said, "Mr. Erickson, if you will wait a few moments, your eyes will be conditioned to the darkness."

He used that story to illustrate that we live in a world where we are little by little being conditioned to the darkness.

May we never be conditioned to the darkness of this world!

MIRACLES

The month was January, and I was scheduled for a ladies retreat in Danville, Illinois. I was living in Florida at the time and was set to fly from St. Petersburg, Florida, to Chicago, Illinois, and then on to Danville on a small commuter plane.

Upon arrival in Chicago, we had to walk from the plane to the terminal through six inches of snow. A blizzard had hit the state of Illinois, and when we arrived at the terminal, we found out that all commuter flights had been cancelled. The passengers were in an uproar. Angry men and women were shouting at the ticket agents.

I waited in line for an available telephone to call the lady in charge of the retreat to inform her of the situation. I told her that I would not be able to get to Danville that evening as scheduled. She told me that if I could get to any nearby airport they would send someone to transport me to the retreat center. She also told me that the ladies who were already at the retreat would begin praying.

I proceeded to the ticket counter where so many angry passengers had been yelling and screaming at the ticket agent, and I saw that she was close to tears. I just took her hand and said, "Honey, it is okay. It is not your fault." She burst into tears.

A decision was made to allow one flight out and it was going to Evansville, Indiana. I told the ticket agent I would take that flight if there was room and she said, "Dear, I will put you on that flight ahead of all the others." I called the lady in charge of the retreat and updated her. She told me they would have someone with a 4-wheel drive pick me up when I landed.

When we boarded the plane, the man beside me was still angry and using foul language. I said, "Sir, don't take my Lord's name in vain. I am upset also, but that kind of language will get you nowhere. Now, just relax and bow your head. I am going to pray." I prayed that God would get us safely to our destinations and that he would calm my friend beside me, thanked the Lord, and then said "Amen." I immediately went to sleep.

I woke up and heard the pilot saying, "Fasten your seat belts tightly and put your head between your legs. We are making an emergency landing."

As we braced ourselves for the emergency landing, I looked out the window and saw the terminal sign. We were landing in Danville, Illinois! When my seatmate saw the sign he said, "Oh, great, Danville, Illinois." I said, "This is where I am supposed to be." His eyes were wide and he said, "Lady, who are you?" And I replied, "Only a Servant of the Lord."

I called the lady in charge of the retreat and told her I was at the airport. She told me that someone was on the way to Evansville to get me. I said, "No, I am at the Danville, Illinois Airport."

I found out later that the plane's wings had become too heavy with ice, thus the forced landing, and that over fifty ladies had been on their knees praying for me. WHAT A MIGHTY GOD WE SERVE!

JUST STAY IN THE RACE

"I have fought the good fight, I have finished the race, I have kept the faith. 8 Now there is in store for me the crown of righteousness, which the Lord, the righteous Judge, will award to me on that day —and not only to me, but also to all who have longed for his appearing." II Timothy 4:7-8 (NIV)

Ben-Hur is my all-time favorite movie. I watch the reruns each time it is shown on TV. I have the video and my daughter even gave me tickets to see the live performance.

Charlton Heston plays the lead part of Judah Ben-Hur, and who could ever forget the exciting chariot race? Charlton Heston worked very hard for many weeks to be able to really ride and to stand up in the chariot. He finally went to the producer, and said, "Sir, I have worked diligently to be able to ride the chariot, and I think I can drive, but I am not sure I can win the race." The producer smiled and said, "Charlton, you just stay in the race, and I will see that you win."

Footnote: *The Lord says to each of us, "'Just stay in the race, and I will see that you win the race."*

IN THE FATHER'S HAND

"...no one can snatch them out of my hand." John 10:28 (NIV)

This Scripture will always hold a special place in my life as God gave it to me when I was at one of the lowest points in my life.

We were hurting so badly because my husband had been asked to resign from the ministry. I was minister of music at the same church, so two excellent salaries were cut overnight. Through the years I have tried to be frugal, but now it was especially necessary to watch every penny.

It was such a grief-stricken time, and we both were very fragile. Over and over we cried out to the Lord to open some door for ministry to us. But God was silent.

One day I stopped by the day-old bread store to pick up a loaf of bread. When I got back in the car, the car wouldn't start. This was before the days of cell phones. What did we ever do without them? I had to walk across a busy street to get to the pay phone so that I could have Elvin come and help me. There was no answer.

I was in the poor district of the city. I went back to the car and rolled up the windows and locked the doors. I made three more attempts at calling my husband. Still, there was no answer. After the third time, I just draped myself across the steering wheel and sobbed. A man knocked on the window and asked if I was all right, but I was afraid to trust anyone in this part of town. When I got tired of crying, I saw an old *Our Daily Bread* devotional book on the passenger's seat. I picked it up and opened it to a devotional with the Scripture John 10:28. Satan blinded my eyes to the Word at that moment, but the story that followed would forever change my pity party.

The story was about a young woman whose husband had left her with three small children. She had no job, no income, and had asked the church to help her many times. But on this day, she was so discouraged she wanted to commit suicide. She didn't know what the children would do without her, so she called her pastor, and said, "Can you come? I am at the end of my rope and I want to take my life." The pastor told her he would be right there. When he arrived, she was holding the baby in her arms. He said, "Throw your baby on the floor." She said, "Pastor, are you crazy? I wouldn't throw my baby on the floor." To which the pastor replied, "I will pay your bills for the next three months if you will just throw your baby on the floor." She was appalled that he would even say such a thing. She cried out, "I could never throw my baby on the floor." The pastor stated, "Then what makes you think that your Heavenly Father would ever let you go?" He then quoted to her

John 10:28—"No one can snatch them out of my hand."

It was a direct message from the Lord to me. Instead of the car being a place of doom for me that afternoon, it became a sanctuary to praise the Lord. No matter what was going on in my life, He would never let me go. Nor will He let any Christian go from His mighty and loving arms.

P.S. Elvin did finally answer the phone.

AIN'T WORKIN'

I have five grandsons. I enjoyed spending special one-on-one time with each of them. When Andy was small, he was spending the night with me. We first started out playing Nintendo. It was short-lived since I could not remember to use two hands instead of one. We then played some more games, and since I was getting sleepy, I said, "Let's lie down on the couch, and I will read to you." I was thinking he might be sleepy but guess who got sleepy? I said, "Andy, Ba is getting sleepy. Can we go to bed?" Andy replied, "Yes, but would you sleep with me?" I said, "Sure."

We were in the bathroom brushing our teeth, and I put some cold cream on my face. He was watching all of this and said, "What is that greasy stuff?" I told him it was cold cream, and it would help me take off my makeup.

I then put on the night cream. Again he asked, "What is that greasy stuff?" I said, "Honey, this is night cream, and it keeps me from getting wrinkles." He said, "Ba, it ain't workin."

Thanks, Andy, for a child's insight. I have shared this story from the platform many times.

JESUS LIVES INSIDE OF ME

"Christ in you, the hope of glory." Colossians 1:27 (NIV)

The pastor's sermon was based on Colossians 1:27 which stated to everyone that the hope of His glory would be that Christ lives in each of us.

A little girl listened intently. On the way home from church, she said to her daddy, "Daddy, did the pastor say that Jesus lives inside of me?" The father replied, "Yes, honey." In just a few moments she said, "Daddy, how tall is Jesus?" The father said, "Honey, I don't know, probably about your daddy's size." They rode a few more miles; then she said, "Well, if Jesus lives inside of me, He is going to stick out all over."

That is a true statement. If Jesus lives inside of us, He is going to stick out all over.

GOD'S PROTECTION

"For he will command his angels concerning you." Psalm 91:11 (NIV)

Prayer is always a must before I leave my home for any scheduled engagement. It has been a joy to share the platform with my daughter, Love Lockman. She is the minister's wife at Seymour Christian Church, Seymour, Indiana.

Love and I were scheduled to speak for a ladies retreat in Illinois. Before we left home, we prayed for God's protection and for God to use us to His glory.

It was raining as we left our homes for the three-hour drive. About one hour into our journey, a downpour occurred. It was almost impossible to see the highway. Many cars had already pulled off the highway. Love did the same and waited until she had more visibility. We were off the highway for just a few minutes when she said, "I don't know why I did that. My husband, a former policeman, always says to put on your flashers and keep driving slowly." So she pulled back on the highway. We had only gone a short distance when we came upon a terrible accident. Why had we pulled off the highway? We both gulped and shed a few tears. God knew why she had pulled off the highway for those few minutes. It was for our protection.

Thank you, Lord, for your command of your angels to watch over me for those thousands of miles I have traveled for you.

KEEP YOUR HANDS TO YOURSELF

When we ministered in Brownstown, Indiana, the closest hospital was in Seymour, Indiana. My husband was at the hospital almost every day visiting the sick. At that time there was no chaplain and the ministers of the area took turns being the chaplains on call.

Each Christmas the hospital would hold an appreciation dinner for the chaplains. On this particular formal evening, we were seated at the head table and the Catholic priest asked Elvin to give the blessing for the food and the invocation. Heads were all bowed, and I just wanted my husband to know how proud I was of him. I reached over, under the tablecloth, and squeezed his knee during the prayer. I must also tell you my husband was very ticklish, and when I squeezed his knee he said, "Heavenly Father, wheeeee!" I have no idea if he thanked the Lord for the food or what, but all eyes were on him when he said "Amen."

I grabbed the microphone and said, "My husband does not normally get the Spirit in the middle of the prayer. I wanted him to know I was proud of him, so I squeezed his knee during the prayer." Everyone got a good laugh except Elvin who was quite embarrassed.

Moral of this story: Preacher's wives, when your husband is praying, keep your hands to yourself!

WHY WAS I JUST 'BORNDED'

"For he chose us in him before the creation of the world to be holy and blameless in his sight. In love he predestined us to be adopted as his sons through Jesus Christ." Ephesians 1:4-5a (NIV)

When Love was four years old, she had been playing with her friend who lived next door. She came home sobbing. I stopped what I was doing and took her on my lap and said, "What is wrong? What happened?" Through her tears she answered, "How come you just 'bornded' me?"

I said, "Honey, I don't know what you are talking about. What do you mean, that I just 'bornded' you?" She said, "Well, Tressa said she was 'dopted' and I was just 'bornded' and that she was picked out 'cause she was 'dopted' and since I was just 'bornded' you had to take what you got." I had to choke back a laugh, and I said, "Honey, you were just 'bornded' but we don't love you any less than Tressa who was picked out and 'dopted.'"

This story brings Ephesians 1:4 to my mind: "That we were picked out and 'dopted' into His Kingdom." Thank you, Lord, I was 'dopted.'

RETREATS ARE JUST LIKE HEAVEN

A lady once told me that retreats are just like Heaven. When I asked her why, she said, "There's no night there."

If you have ever been at a campground for a ladies retreat, you know that is a true statement.

BLACK DOG/WHITE DOG

"I've banked your promises in the vault of my heart so I won't sin myself bankrupt."
Psalm 119:11 (The Message)

"I have hidden your word in my heart that I might not sin against you." Psalm
119:11 (NIV)

A man owned a black dog and a white dog. Each Saturday he brought his
two dogs to the town square for a dogfight. Men of the community anxious-
ly awaited the event in order to place their bets on the winning dog.

One week the black dog won and possibly the next week the white dog
won, but no one could ever predict which dog would win. Finally, one of
the men asked the owner of the dogs, "Do you know which dog is going to
win?" The owner replied, "Yes, I do." The gentleman then asked, "How do
you know which one is going to win?" He replied, "The dog I feed all week."

Footnote: *Spiritual food from His Word will make sure the right dog wins.*

LOOK MOMMY, SHE'S HOLLOW

A mother took her young daughter to the local drugstore for an ice-
cream cone. As they were leaving the daughter said, "Mommy, can we
weigh ourselves?" The mother replied, "Let me see if I have a penny." While
the mother was looking for a penny, a large lady stepped on the scales and
put in her penny. The scale's dial went around several times with a swish,
swish, swish, and stopped on two pounds. The daughter was all eyes and
said to her mother, "Look Mommy, she's hollow."

Footnote: Do others see me as hollow?

MRS. HARDY IS FINE

*"Now we know that if the earthly tent we live in is destroyed, we have a building
from God, an eternal house in heaven, not built by human hands."*
II Corinthians 5:1 (NIV)

During my sixty plus years in the ministry, the Lord has placed many
wonderful Christian saints in my path to encourage me in my Christian
journey.

Our first ministry was located in the small town of Lexington, Indiana.
I was a young, inexperienced preacher's wife. Mrs. Ella Hardy was one of

the dear older ladies of that congregation. She provided me a spiritual gem that I have never forgotten. She was not well physically, but she had a sweet, constant smile on her face and a kind word for everyone.

Once, after a dog bit her, she was in the Lord's house on the Lord's Day. I said to her, "Mrs. Hardy, how are you?" She replied, "Oh, Mrs. Hardy's tent is not very well today, but Mrs. Hardy is fine."

YOU SMELL LIKE JESUS

"...through us spreads everywhere the fragrance of the knowledge of him."
II Corinthians 2:14 (NIV)

One time when we were docked at an island on a Caribbean cruise, others were going ashore, but I opted to stay on board. I had been to this island many times, so I decided to go to the top deck for some sun and put the finishing touches on my evening message. I was enjoying the brief time alone when I saw another lady from our Christian group on the top deck. Not knowing her name, only her face, I said, "Are you not going ashore to-day?" She replied, "No, I really do not have the extra money for the tours." I then asked her to join me. I said, "I am sorry, but I do not know your name." She told me her name, and I asked her to tell me about herself. She replied, "Well, there is really not much to tell. I have no family and as you know, I came alone."

We visited for some time, and she told me how much she had always wanted to go on a cruise. Then she said, "My husband and I always dreamed of going on a cruise. He passed away about four years ago. I scraped enough money together to be able to fulfill his dream." I told her how sorry I was, and then she said, "Oh, that is all right, I have Jesus."

She noticed I had my Bible and my notes, and she said, "I don't want to disturb you." I assured her that I wanted to visit with her. She then asked, "What is the message for the evening service?" I replied, "II Corinthians 2:14, that we are to spread the fragrance of Jesus wherever we go and what-ever trials or circumstances we face, that other people will know we spread His fragrance." I said, "You just spread the fragrance of Christ to me when you told me that the death of your husband was all right and that you had Jesus."

She paused a few minutes and tears came to her eyes, and she said, "I so want to do that, Mrs. Gray, but I have lost my husband and three children. One son was killed in a car accident, another died in the Armed Service, and my third child was shot. Mrs. Gray, I can still say, it is all right for they all knew Jesus, and I know they are safely in His arms."

I reached over and took her hand, called her by name, and said, "You smell like Jesus." She said, "What?" I replied, "Yes, I cannot imagine losing a husband and three children and yet you can tell me it is all right." She then said, "Mrs. Gray, I truly can say all is well with my soul. It still hurts, but all is well."

I asked her permission to tell her story to others. Regardless of our circumstances we can say, "It is well with my soul," and to me that's what it means to truly smell like Jesus.

Through the years I have met many who smell like Jesus. I could not begin to list the names, but I smell Jesus in a caregiver when a handicapped child is cared for, or when someone lives with an unsaved mate, or when a parent loves a wayward child, or when someone has gone through a hurtful divorce, or when someone has a loved one in prison, or has to say goodbye to a loved one. Yet, through it all, one remains faithful.

God bless each of you for smelling like Jesus to me.

LOVE LESSONS

"A merry heart doeth good like a medicine." Proverbs 17:22

I taught piano lessons to help with our income for many years, and I taught both Elvina and Love piano lessons. Love was the tomboy and hated practicing the piano. She would much rather be out climbing trees or making mud pies.

When it is your own children you are teaching the lessons to, it is much easier to let the scheduled time slip. On this particular day I said to Love, "I don't care what happens, today is your lesson."

Now the side door of our home was where teenagers could come and go freely. But one day some teenagers walked in and found I was not dressed. From that day, the rule of the house was, teenagers were free to walk in but they must knock first.

I had just started a piano lesson with Love when a knock came at the side door. Thinking it was one of teens I said, "Come in." There was a second knock and I said a little louder, "Come in." I could not see the side door from the piano, so with the third knock I got up to see who was at the door.

It was a strange man and woman that I had not seen before. He said, "We are your new neighbors that just moved in up the street. We were taking a walk, heard the piano music, and thought we would just stop by to introduce ourselves. But if you are busy, we will come back later."

I had seen the moving van and had planned to bake something and welcome them to the neighborhood, but had not done so. I was embarrassed that they came to me first, so I said, "Oh no, I was not busy. I was just giving Love lessons."

The man asked me three times what I was doing and each time I told him, "I'm giving Love lessons and I can do that at any time."

Finally, looking at his wife he said, (remember I had never met this man) "Honey, if she is giving love lessons, why don't you go on home and I will go in."

I started telling this story from the platform when I started speaking around the country. Much to Love's embarrassment when she traveled with the Come Alive Singers from Cincinnati Bible College, ladies would say, "Oh, we know about you. You are the Love of the 'Love Lesson story.'"

MOTHER WOULD

"Train a child in the way he should go, and when he is old he will not turn from it."
Proverbs 22:6 (NIV)

When we were ministering in Brownstown, Indiana, a young mother, Jackie Haubry, fell down the basement stairs in her home. Their young son found her and ran to the office next door to tell his father. The ambulance driver took her to the hospital in Indianapolis, Indiana. My husband went immediately to the hospital to be with her husband, Frank, and to pray.

We called a 24-hour prayer vigil at the church, which meant that someone would be at the church praying for Jackie's recovery every hour for the next few days and nights.

It was a Wednesday evening when we got the word that Jackie had gone on to her heavenly reward. She was the mother of four small children. The entire church family and community were in mourning. We were surprised that evening when we saw her children walking to the Wednesday night prayer meeting. My husband said to the children, "I will take you home tonight, since I want to spend the night with your father." As my husband took the children home, he said to Frank, "I was surprised to see your children at the prayer meeting tonight." Frank replied, "The children went upstairs and got ready for church on their own. When I saw them ready to go with their Bibles in their hands, I said, 'Oh, I don't expect you to go tonight.' To which one of the children replied, 'No, Daddy, we know you don't expect us to go tonight, but Mother would.'"

Frank said, "With a lump in my throat, I watched them walk out the door and off to the church.'"

HE FORGIVES YOU

"Though your sins are like scarlet, they shall be as white as snow; though they are red as crimson, they shall be like wool." Isaiah 1:18b (NIV)

Many years ago before abortion became legalized, I was invited to a college campus to give three lectures against legalizing abortion. I had done my homework and was into my final lecture of why abortion was against God's law. During my last lecture, I was making my closing remarks, and really wanting to emphasize what an important issue this was to us and to our God. Right then, the Lord spoke to me. God does not speak to me audibly, but to my heart, and it was so strong I just stopped. Then I said, "The Lord has placed on my heart that someone in this room has had an abortion. And God wants me to tell you that He loves you and you are forgiven." Then I went on with the closing remarks of the lecture. The flesh is always a little embarrassed when I do that.

Following the lecture, a young woman was waiting to talk to me. I could tell she had been crying, and I took her behind the platform curtain and held her for a few minutes while she sobbed and said, "I am that woman."

She said, "No one knows my story except my preacher, my husband, and me." She then told me she was a young teenage girl in her church youth group and fell in love with the youth minister of the church. She became pregnant and she knew it would ruin her future husband's ministry and her reputation, so they went over the state line where she had an abortion. They told no one. She said, " My wedding day was one of the saddest days of my life, and we have never forgiven ourselves for what we did. Did God really place on your heart that someone was in the audience that had an abortion?" I assured her that He did, and that I was really a little embarrassed that I had stopped the lecture to say that. She said, "Do you really think God still loves me and that He can forgive me for taking an innocent life?" God gave me these words to say to her, "My dear, I also killed an innocent life." She said, "You did?" "Yes," I replied, "I killed the most innocent man who ever lived, Jesus, and it was because of my sins that I killed him. If He has forgiven me, He has also forgiven you."

It was as though a heavy load had been lifted. She could not thank me enough. I asked her to thank God, as He loved her so much that He asked me to stop in the closing of my lecture to give her this direct message.

Footnote: Thank you, Lord, for your blood that cleanses us from all our sins.

UNTIL HE LOVES ME BACK

My daughter Love had physical complications at the birth of their first son, and my first grandson, Billy.

I was already planning to help during this exciting time, but Billy made his appearance into this world earlier than we had anticipated. It was the time of the year for mother/daughter banquets, and I was scheduled to speak every evening of that week.

Love was not allowed to lift Billy, so before I left for the banquet I placed Billy in her arms. Love and I were just amazed at how God had given us this precious new life.

I said, "Is this not the most beautiful child you have ever seen?" Love's response, "Oh Mother, I love him so much already, but I just can't wait until he loves me back."

As I drove to the banquet, those words kept ringing in my ear, "I just can't wait until he loves me back." The thought came to me, I wonder how many times God thinks that of us?

"What Can Wash Away My Sins? Nothing But the Blood of Jesus."

While ministering in Julesburg, Colorado, the telephone rang at the parsonage very early one Sunday morning. My husband jumped out of bed to answer the phone. He then quickly dressed to go to the home of Buck and Mary Newton.

There have been many conversion stories in our ministry, but Buck Newton was one of those dramatic changes and stories of one giving their life to the Lord.

Buck had a beautiful baritone voice, and when I found this out from his teenage daughter Nancy, I asked him to sing in church with his daughter.

Now Buck was the town blacksmith and had a reputation as the town's gambler and drinker. He would work all day and gamble on the blacksmith floor most of the night. His wife worked to keep bread on the table.

At first he was reluctant to sing in church, but with much nudging from me and his daughter, he said that he would sing with Nancy, the 'apple of his eye.'

I had them scheduled to sing during a church revival. It was that night that Buck Newton heard the gospel message and came down the aisle and gave his life to the Lord.

My husband would go by the town blacksmith shop each day to encourage Buck, and now instead of where drinking and gambling had taken place, the blacksmith shop became a place for prayer meetings. The entire town was talking about this change.

When my husband got to the home that Sunday morning, Buck's little grandbaby had quit breathing. My husband, being a former medic in the Army, gave the child mouth-to-mouth resuscitation, but it was too late.

While my husband was doing so, the medic arrived. They began the same procedure, but the medics said, "it is too late". The child had died of crib-death.

My husband tried to console the family and then said, "Buck, did you call me before you called the medics?"

He replied, "Yes."

My husband said, "But why would you call me first, Buck?"

His reply, "Preacher, you were the one who gave me life."

Footnote: Buck became such a dear friend. My girls adored him. He gave an Easter egg hunt for the entire community. My girls called him "Bucka' Newton."

THE FAITH HEALER

When I first began speaking, it was not uncommon for me to speak several times in one week. There might be close connections on flights or driving, but I was on the platform and wanted to be used of God in as many ways as possible.

I had spoken in West Virginia and caught my flight on a commuter plane, which I hate, into Cincinnati, Ohio, where I was speaking the next day at Cincinnati Bible College, now called Cincinnati Christian University. The lady who had invited me to the Bible College knew my schedule and had arranged for someone to pick me up at the airport and take me to the college. At that time our daughter Love was a student at Cincinnati Bible College and she knew my schedule. Since it was going to be late, we had already discussed that I would see her the next morning because I would be arriving past her curfew.

The plane from West Virginia had been in a storm and air turbulence was a nail-biter. It was all I could do to keep my stomach right side up. When I finally landed at the airport, tired and nauseous, I heard the song *Rock of Ages*. Standing on the benches in the airport were my daughter Love and several of her buddies from the college singing *Rock of Ages* at the top of their lungs. There was also a large sign they had made which said, "LOOKING FOR BETTY GRAY, THE FAITH HEALER."

I was hoping to ignore the entire mess, but then one young man had his leg wrapped in bandages, another was on crutches, and they knelt in front of me and yelled, "Heal me, heal me!"

I would have ignored them or acted like I didn't know them, but I had to wait for my luggage from the commuter plane at that very location. I couldn't just fade into the woodwork. As we were leaving the airport, people were pointing at me and whispering, "There she is, there she is."

Thanks, Love, for a forever memory!

SILLY GRANDMOTHER

Billy was my first-born grandson. I never thought I would be one of those silly grandmothers, but I must have been quite obnoxious. To experience being a grandparent was beyond anything I could have ever imagined!

I always stood with my husband at the front door following the morning services to shake hands with all those in attendance. After Billy was born, I had someone scheduled to go to the church nursery and bring him to me, so everyone could see the preacher's new grandson and this amazing baby. Sunday after Sunday the congregation would 'oooh' and 'ahhh' over Billy. He became a permanent attraction at the front door.

Now you need to know that he was one of the cutest and smartest children that ever lived. When he was old enough to talk, I would tell the people to ask Billy what he was going to be when he grew up. I then whispered in his ear and said, "a preacher." He would say "preacher" and they would all smile and remark on how precious that was. He was already counting to ten and saying his ABC's at a very young age.

I scheduled a date with Billy at least once a week. We generally went to 'Donald's' for a Happy Meal. One day, I had just picked him up and was driving down the highway to our date, and I decided we needed to rehearse so that I would not need to whisper in his ear each Sunday as to what he was going to do when he grew up.

I said, "Billy, what are you going to be when you grow up?" He had a blank look on his face and I repeated, "Billy, each Sunday morning the people ask you what you are going to be when you grow up, and I want you to learn to answer without my having to tell you. What are you going to be when you grow up?" Wanting to please me he said, "Go potty?"

When Billy was 16 years old, I put this story on video in the drama GRANNY, and I am not sure he has forgiven me.

YOUR ARM HAS COME UNSCREWED

My sister-in-law, Ann Gray, tells a story that I have used many times from the platform.

When her grandson Kyle was a little boy, she was rocking him and loving on him, and Kyle began to give his grandmother love pats in return. When he started to pat under her arms, he said, "Did you know your arm has come unscrewed?"

Anyone over fifty years of age will understand this story.

ORGAN PLAYING - HAWAIIAN STYLE

My husband was always volunteering me to be on the platform sometimes without my approval, but he knew I didn't mind.

The Ministerial Association was planning a combined community Thanksgiving service, and since my husband was the chairman of the Association, he was responsible for the program. At the Association meeting everyone had volunteered to take part in the program, and they said, "We need someone to play the organ." My husband said, "My wife will be glad to play the organ."

He had given me ample time to go to this hosting church to practice on their organ, and since he had given me a list of songs, I felt I could handle it without a problem.

When the evening came, I had my outline and my responsibilities and all my music in order. I was to play a prelude, and then at the appointed time I was to increase the volume for the processional as each of the community ministers came to the platform.

I had never played a Lowry organ but used the pre-sets and had no problem until it came time for the processional. I put my foot on the expression pedal to increase the volume. What I did not know was that a Lowry organ has a Hawaiian attachment that is to the left of the expression pedal. As the ministers came down the aisle, I hit the Hawaiian button, and it would have been appropriate for the ministers to have done the hula dance down the aisle.

I had no idea what was causing the Hawaiian music, but I could hardly hold back a laugh as I could picture the ministers in grass skirts.

A LITTLE PAINT NEVER HURT ANY BARN

When we first started in the ministry sixty years ago, I did not realize how critical church people could be of the preacher's wife.

One lady came up to my husband and said, "Do you know that Betty is wearing make-up?" Elvin told her he did. She said, "I don't think that it is appropriate for a preacher's wife to wear make-up." My husband patiently said, "Have you ever seen Betty without her make-up?" She then replied, "No, I haven't." Elvin said, "Then you must remember that a little paint never hurt any barn."

IT TAKES MORE LOVE TO LET HER GO

Elvin was patient and understanding when the Lord opened up the speaking ministry to me. Many ministers asked him, "How do you handle your wife being gone so much?" He would just say, "I love to wind her up and watch her go."

At one ladies retreat a lady came to me and said, "Do you travel like this every weekend?" I assured her that I did, and then she said, "Well, my husband loves me too much to let me be gone."

All the way home I kept thinking about those words. Maybe he likes it when I am gone. When I got home I was always walking on the clouds and sharing with him the entire weekend of how God had blessed it. After this remark I was feeling pretty glum.

Elvin said, "What is the matter? Did the retreat not go well?" Finally I told him what this lady had said. He said, "Sit down. I want you to know it takes a lot more love to let you be gone than it does for you to stay home. Don't you ever forget that."

Yes, I continued traveling, so he could love me more!

DON'T SQUEEZE THE CHARMIN

I was speaking at Florida Christian College Ladies Day near Kissimmee, Florida. The evening before the all-day event, the college provided a motel room for me.

I needed to get a good night of rest and was just ready to retire when I discovered I had not packed the satin protector for my teased hair. You young girls have no idea what we went through years ago. The higher the tease, the more hair spray you needed, and the more fashionable you were.

I needed to look my best on the platform in front of hundreds of ladies that were coming from across the state. I had no protector. What was I going to do?

I went to the bathroom and wrapped my teased hair with the old trick of toilet paper. I had no bobby pins to keep it in place and as I lay down, soon it was on my pillow.

So I got out of bed and saw a shower cap. I wrapped my head in toilet paper and then put on the shower cap. It stayed in place wonderfully, and I had a good night of sleep.

I had set my alarm for 4:00 a.m. to go over my messages and to under-gird myself with prayer. When I took off the shower cap, it had acted just like a sauna, and my hair was wet with the toilet paper stuck to my hair. My beauty-salon teased hair, with a can of hair spray, was ruined! I used the hair pick to see if I could get the toilet paper out, but with the hair spray it was there to stay.

There was a sign on the motel mirror that said, "If you have forgotten anything, call the front desk." I dialed the front desk and said, "I have for-gotten my hair dryer." To which the lady said, "I am the only one here, but if you will come to the front desk, I will give you a hair dryer." I replied, "I can't. I have toilet paper in my hair." Click. She hung up on me. Can you imagine what she was thinking?

Suddenly a knock comes at the door, and here is the young lady with the hair dryer. With wide eyes she said, "You do have toilet paper in your hair!"

I did the best I could. Thank goodness my hair had already started to turn white, so if there was still any toilet paper, possibly they thought it was just hair turning white.

One of the young ladies that came on the bus from the church said, "If you don't mind, I'd like to ride home with you." I told her that would be fine. The more I thought about the incident of the toilet paper the funnier it got, so I told her the story on our way home. Her remark, "Mrs. Gray, you ap-pear to be so intelligent."

I was not going to tell this story to anyone, as that was pretty stupid. But my daughter Love called that evening and wanted to know all about the weekend. Love has a crazy sense of humor like I do, so I told her the story.

She thought it was hilarious, but I was going to let this story die because I did not want to appear unintelligent.

What I did not know was that Elvin had heard me tell the story to Love. He had not said a word to me, but Monday morning when I went in to the staff meeting of the church, the minister of education said, "I do believe when any of us from the church appear in public that we should be careful how we look." Well, I was the only woman on staff and was supposing one of them had done something embarrassing, and then he said, "Especially if you have toilet paper in your hair." My husband had related the story to the entire staff at my expense. I was called CHARMIN in that congregation for many months.

That morning after staff meeting as I was going out the door for lunch, the youth minister, Mark Frenier, said, "I have this uncontrollable urge to squeeze you." Remember that old Charmin commercial?

Q-U-E-E-N SIZE

A lady in Michigan said, "Betty, I have a great grandmother story you can tell across the country." Here is the story. A six year old went to the grocery store with his grandmother. He wanted to get in the grocery cart and the grandmother said, "No, I can no longer lift you." He said, "I can climb in." The grandmother replied, "No, I have too many groceries to get today. You may hang on the front or walk here with me."

He was mad at his grandmother because he didn't get his way. He was pouting and hanging on the front of the cart. The first item that the grandmother placed in the cart was a pair of panty hose. Now we all know that children at six years of age are just learning to spell and pronounce words. So to embarrass his grandmother he began to spell loudly off the panty hose package, "Q-U-E-E-N," and then he tries to sound it out. "QU- QUEE-QUEEN." The grandmother said, "Be quiet, everyone is looking at us."

He then proceeded to loudly spell " S-I-Z-E," and to sound out this word. The grandmother said, "Stop it, you are embarrassing me."

He said, "Grandmother, are you going to wear those?" She answered, "Yes, I am going to wear those." The grandson said, "But Grandma, queen size, did you know you are the same size as my mattress?"

HONORS

TO GOD BE THE GLORY

Many honors have been bestowed upon me during my sixty plus years in the ministry. I never dreamed what God had in store for this little country girl.

The churches we served embraced me as a partner in ministry with my husband; for this I am honored.

In ministry I have done many things far beyond my own ability. I give all the honor and credit to the Lord.

Many times when I get on a platform, an overwhelming feeling will overtake me. You know, that 'What am I doing here?' feeling. My prayer is always, "Lord, you know these hearts and their needs. I do not. May I get out of the way so you can speak."

Now, in the later years, my added prayer is, "Lord, may fresh water flow through these rusty pipes."

To each platform in the states and foreign countries where I have stood, I am honored.

For the writing and directing of the musicals and large productions, such as Living Christmas Trees and the Easter pageants, which were far beyond my ability, I have always stood in awe of what God has done. And for this I am honored.

To the ladies retreats around the world, I thank my God for using me in this way. I am humbled and honored.

For the past thirty years of drama ministry, I have asked God to give me the drama that was needed, and he has given that, and so much more. For this I am so humbled and honored.

I am grateful and honored for the protection God has given me in Haiti and other foreign mission fields.

I am also grateful for God's protection as I traveled thousands of miles through the years.

80TH BIRTHDAY CELEBRATION

I turned 80 years of age on January 11, 2010. I had already told my daughter Love, with tongue in cheek, that I really expected a big celebration.

Without my knowledge, Bill Lockman, my son-in-law and Kyle Brown, our church technician, from Seymour Christian Church, hacked into my e-mails, which number over one thousand, and sent a note inviting everyone to my surprise 80th birthday celebration.

Elvina and her family came from Georgia, and my grandson Andy and his family came from Florida. We all sat together for the morning worship service, and I was recognized from the platform for my birthday. We had what I thought was my celebration.

Following Sunday morning services, I took my family out to eat at a nice restaurant.

I was intent on getting group pictures and had the waiter take pictures of all the family. I thought everyone was leaving for their own homes. What I did not know was that they all went to the church to decorate for my party.

My daughter Love said, "We are picking you up at 6:00 p.m. to go to dinner for your birthday." I told her, "No, we have already celebrated my birthday." But she insisted and said, "Be sure to dress nicely as we are going to a nice restaurant." She would not take no for an answer.

Reluctantly, I was ready by 6:00 p.m. The doorbell rang, and there stood all five of my grandsons on the front porch, and a stretch limousine waiting out front.

When we got in the limo I said, "Where are we going?" and my grandson Billy said, "Oh Ba, we are taking you in style to the nearest nursing home."

Instead, they took me in style to the church where a large crowd of family and friends were waiting to celebrate my birthday. People from seven states were in attendance.

I was escorted to the platform as my dear friend and recording artist, Julie

Nevel was playing, *Cruisin' with Betty,* on the piano. This was an original and humorous song she had written regarding my push to get her on a cruise ship.

I was presented with many gifts and over one thousand letters and cards that were sent from across the country.

Many people gave testimonies of what my life had meant to them. A special surprise testimony came from my dear friend, Sharyl Bledsoe, from Texas. This was a tearful, yet amazing evening of honor.

BETTY GRAY SCHOLARSHIP FOR WOMEN

For this 80th birthday celebration, Johnson Bible College, Knoxville, Tennessee, now Johnson University, established The Betty Gray Scholarship Fund for Women. This is a scholarship for women wanting to go into full-time ministry who may otherwise not be able to afford the education and training to do so.

I know it is hard to believe, but I was speechless on the platform.

FAMILY

My family is the greatest honor that the Lord has given me. Especially now in my sunset years, I am so humbled that God entrusted me with two beautiful daughters and two wonderful, dedicated Christian sons-in-law.

There is no greater joy than to see both of my girls raise their sons in the way of the Lord and to see them both serving the Lord.

God has blessed me with five grandsons. And as my grandsons find their soul mates, I am looking forward to finally having granddaughters.

When I was interviewed in Australia for a radio program, the station manager looked at my resume and said, "Mrs. Gray, what is the greatest accomplishment in your life?" I thought for a moment and said, "My greatest accomplishment is not on that paper, but my greatest accomplishment is raising two daughters in the way of the Lord."

Thank you, Lord, for thinking of family.

Footnote: I am trying to be good to my family, as I know they will be selecting the nursing home for me.

GRAND MARSHALL

Pekin, Indiana, has held the longest, continual Fourth of July celebration in the nation.

In 2000 I was selected by the Pekin Parade Committee to be the Grand Marshall of the parade. They requested that I dress as BETSY ROSS. It was 100 degrees that day, but I knew Elvin Gray was smiling down from heaven because his wife would be so honored to be the Grand Marshall of the Pekin Fourth of July parade.

You see, one of my husband's fondest childhood memories was attending the annual celebration and Fourth of July parade in Pekin, Indiana.

GOD'S SILENT SERVANTS

Mary responded, "I am the Lord's servant. May everything you have said about me come true." And then the angel left her. Luke 1:38 (NLT)

"And my God will meet all your needs according to his glorious riches in Christ Jesus." Philippians 4:19 (NIV)

I am so honored to know so many of God's silent servants. I cannot begin to list all who have played such a vital part of this platform ministry. I would like to list a few.

Don and Virginia Dugan have labored with me for over thirty years as two of God's most dedicated silent servants. Heaven holds a special place for these two. They believed in me, even when I did not believe in myself.

Don and Virginia have spent countless hours assisting and arranging my bookings, correspondence, receipts, newsletters, mailings, financials, and taking care of other personal needs. People all across the country tell me how they enjoy their phone conversations when they call for bookings and hope to meet them one day.

Thank you, Don and Virginia, for being God's silent servants. I am honored and humbled to have you as my fellow laborers and friends.

DRIVER SHARYL

After my dear husband's death, God provided Sharyl Powers Bledsoe as a driver. Sharyl, a Georgia schoolteacher, came to Indiana during the summer months to be my driver. She was not only my driver, but also my dear friend. We shared so many laughs and tears together.

I had her kissing many a 'frog' before she met her prince charming, Dell Bledsoe. He had the nerve to move her to the state of Texas. Needless to say, she was no longer my traveling buddy but has remained a cherished, forever friend.

DRIVER BEV

I never cease to marvel at how God supplies all of my needs according to His riches in glory. Now that I am in life's sunset years, I am so thankful that God brought Bev Gaiter to me.

Bev Gaiter served as secretary at the Brownstown Christian Church during our ministry there some thirty years ago.

As secretary, when she would place something on the minister's desk she would just place her initials BG on it. Some days I also volunteered in the church office. One day Elvin said to me, "Why are you doing that when we have a secretary?" I had no idea what he was referring to and told him I did not do it. He said, "Your initials, BG, are on this paper." To this day Bev Gaiter is BG, Jr. (junior), and I am BG, Sr. (senior).

Bev later became my driver and assistant.

GOD PROVIDES A COSTUME DESIGNER

I had just started the drama ministry and had only two dramas in my repertoire. A young lady came up to me at a ladies retreat at Camp Northward in Falmouth, Kentucky, and said, "Do you make your costumes?" I laughed and told her that I certainly could not sew and had someone make FANNY CROSBY'S costume and the costume for CORRIE TEN BOOM. She said, "The Lord placed on my heart that I could do that for you." Tonya Babik of Walton, Kentucky, has made over fifteen costumes for the drama ministry, all beautifully hand-made and designed by Tonya. After thirty years, I am still wearing these costumes. Tonya is another of God's silent servants.

PRAYER WARRIORS

"For this reason, since the day we heard about you, we have not stopped praying for you." Colossians 1:9 (NIV)

I have been so blessed through these sixty plus years on the platform to be given the "Gift of Prayer" by many prayer warriors. If hearts have been touched, it was not Betty Gray; it was a result of prayers.

Many times I have said something that really embarrassed my flesh, only to find out afterwards that very statement was what had touched a heart.

I have my team of prayer warriors that know my schedule and pray for me while I am on the platform. Many of whom, I do not even know their names, but God does. I am honored!

RITA RIGLE

Rita, a minister's wife in Logansport, Indiana, loved the Lord and she loved me. When I was speaking within one hundred miles, she was always there. Not only was she always there, but she brought a van full of ladies to hear me on the platform. She called herself, a Betty Gray 'groupie.'

For over ten years, when I arrived at an engagement, there was a letter waiting for me. I knew it would be from Rita, just saying, "I am praying for you." She called the *Encourage Me* office to find out what time I would be on the platform and the name of the person in charge and mailed the card to that address.

For the past several years Rita no longer knows her family or me, and is tenderly cared for by her husband John. Rita was God's silent servant and a prayer warrior that lifted me up while I was on the platform.

GOD'S FAITHFUL PARTNERS

"Always giving thanks to God the Father for everything, in the name of our Lord Jesus Christ." Ephesians 5:20 (NIV)

I am so honored, humbled and thankful for you who have had a partnership with me with your love gifts. Many have been sacrificial and I do not take this lightly. Your gifts have made it possible for me to stay on the platform.

If any lives have been touched and changed, it is because of you. As silent servants, you have made it possible.

JULIE NEVEL

My first introduction to recording artist, Julie Nevel, was at a ladies retreat in Pennsylvania where she shared the program with me. Julie ministered in music, and I was the featured speaker. Just before I was to speak, Julie sang a song she had written entitled *Angel Wings*. I was so touched by the words that I could not control my emotions, and I was weeping when it came time for me to speak.

Angel Wings
The little boy was lonely, the only kid on his street
And even at his Sunday School there weren't many kids to meet
So his worried mother went to find a companion for her son
And the little boy that she brought home was quite a different one
He was kind and friendly with sparkling eyes of blue
But he was crippled, and a hunchback too.

So the worried mother told her son, "Be careful what you say
Don't talk about his differences," and she sent them out to play
The surprise came later when she went to take the boys a snack
And she overheard her son say, "Do you know what that is on your back?"
Well the little hunchback boy just paused and turned away
Then the worried mother heard her little boy say

Chorus
It is the box in which your wings are
And someday you will see
God will cut it open, and you will fly away
You'll be an angel, an angel you will be

No matter what your trial, your thorn in the flesh
God gives sufficient grace and He is there in our distress
When we are weak, our God is strong, our growth is His desire

Impurities are burned away when we go through the fire
The very thing that burdens us might, in the end
Be what perfects us drawing us to Him again.

Words & Music by Julie Nevel, 1992 Nevel Music (Used by permission)

Little did I know at that time that I would minister in various states and foreign countries with this gifted and anointed musician.

MY 'OLDER' FRIEND – HARRIET

Harriet Maynard Aughinbaugh was, and is, one of the most accomplished and gifted pianist I have ever known.

During my years as minister of music at the Central Christian Church, St. Petersburg, Florida, Harriet, along with Joan Hess and Jeannene Hood, volunteered many hours as accompanist to the numerous choirs and ensembles. This is when the revival platform of leading song services, playing the vibraharp, and singing solos was opened to me.

Harriet traveled with me to numerous engagements. We shared many nights in hotel rooms and discovered that we had similar upbringings. We both had godly parents, and we were born in the state of Indiana. We both had a love for music, and we were the same age.

Harriet's birthday is in July and my birthday is in January, so I always assumed I was six months older than she, and she loved to tell people that I was older. Then one evening I said, "Harriet, what year were you born?" It was then that I discovered she was six months older than me! I have never let her forget this.

I introduced her one evening at a revival service as my mother. A fellowship time followed the service, and one lady did not realize I was joking and she said, "Well, now that I see you both up close, I do believe you look older than your mother."

Harriet has been a great example to me and countless others. Just as she and her husband were ready to retire and enjoy life, her husband died a tragic death.

She is now married to Dr. Paul Aughinbaugh, a Presbyterian minister.

After all these years, Harriet still travels to Lake James Christian Assembly in Angola, Indiana, to accompany me for their Dinner Theatre and the Best Years Days.

Harriet, you are my forever buddy and older friend.

SECOND
CHILDHOOD

A time of life where you stop long enough to reflect over the numerous blessings God has given you. A Second Childhood, it is where grown-ups can be kids and be child-like without being childish. Some may call it senility, geezer hood or dotage...but I just call it BLESSINGS. - Betty Gray

SECOND CHILDHOOD

I never dreamed what God had in store for my platform after my beloved husband's death in 1998. Elvin and I worked together in all aspects of the ministry. Although God had already opened up the speaking/drama ministry, I was not sure I could continue without him.

As we traveled in the RV, he unloaded all the equipment, the musical instruments, the costumes, and the set-up for the display. He would then make sure everything was in place and ready for the program.

After the program, while I greeted the people, he 'manned' the display table. Then he loaded the equipment and instruments and slipped up behind me and whispered, "You can stop talking now, everything is loaded."

When his health began to deteriorate, it was evident that he could no longer travel with me. At that time, we were booked for several engagements a week. Now it was my responsibility to load, unload, and man the table.

I vividly remember the first time I did this because self-pity filled my soul. He wanted me to continue the ministry, and I obtained caregivers to stay with him. However, it became increasingly more difficult, because of my deep concern for him.

At a particular engagement, no one could help me unload or load. As I drove away, I just talked to the Lord, "I can't do this." I was just letting the Lord know how sorry I was feeling for myself. I must have vented for about twenty minutes. Then the Lord replied to me. Now the Lord does not speak audibly to me, but on this occasion He spoke to my heart and said, "Betty, why don't you just start thanking me, instead of blaming me?" It was such a strong message from the Lord that I had to pull the van off the road, and tearfully apologize to Him. I always kept a note pad on the passenger seat to record any ideas that I might have. On the three-hour return drive to our home in southern Indiana, I started to write down all my blessings for which I should thank Him.

When I arrived home, I shared this with Elvin and we both cried. Then he said, "Turn that page over and let me add some things to your list." To this day I still have that precious list.

ELVIN'S HOME-GOING

My beloved husband, Elvin, with his body failing, looked forward to his heavenly home. We talked for many hours about his home-going.

For me, it was a bitter-sweet time. At first I didn't want to talk about it, but he had everything planned and wanted to give me instructions of what I was to do when he was no longer with me. For forty-seven years of our married life he always put the Lord first and then me.

He would hear a new song on the radio or television and say, "I want that at my memorial service." He also had asked both of his daughters and me to speak at his home-going service, and that his son-in-law, Bill Lockman would officiate the service.

I told him, "If we have everything you asked for at this memorial service it would last all day." He replied, "That will be fine, as I will not be there."

We did have a beautiful praise service. Elvina, Love, and I spoke at the service. The three of us had all written down what we wanted to say. If we couldn't speak, my son-in-law would read our tributes to him.

To put those who had come for the memorial service at ease, I said, "Elvin asked me to speak and told me, if there is a good crowd, be sure to take up an offering." There was a large crowd, with standing room only at the Bunker Hill Christian Church, Salem, Indiana, but we didn't take up an offering. The family exited the church by everyone standing and singing the great old hymn *How Great Thou Art.*

YOUR MINISTRY WILL INCREASE THREE-FOLD

Following the beautiful memorial service for Elvin, we were leaving the cemetery when the hospice chaplain stopped me. He said, "I have a message from the Lord for you." I am always a little skeptical when someone says that. But he had been such a comfort to us over the past three months, and I respected him greatly. He said, "Your ministry will increase three-fold." He then turned to both of my daughters and said, "You make sure she understands this message," and repeated the message again to them.

When we returned to the house we discussed this strange message.

Prior to Elvin's failing health we always did everything together. Ours was a team ministry, and it was unthinkable that the Lord would increase my ministry three-fold.

Little did I know then that this was a direct message from the Lord.

REMAIN FAITHFUL

"Be faithful, even to the point of death, and I will give you the crown of life." Revelation 2:10b (NIV)

After Elvin's death in October 1998, I had already made plans to go to Florida for the winter months. The *Encourage Me Ministries* office had been asked for two years if I would do a Christmas program at a large trailer park in St. Petersburg, Florida. I was not sure I could do a drama, but since they had asked for two years prior I felt I must try to do it.

Anyone who has lost his/her beloved soul mate knows that empty feeling, and how challenging it is to even put one foot in front of the other one.

At the huge Christmas affair in the recreation hall of the trailer park, the St. Petersburg High School chorus provided the music, and I was asked to present MARY, THE MOTHER OF JESUS as the final act.

When I arrived at the hall, I could tell it was BYOB (bring your own bottle) and by the time I was to go to the platform, many were already wasted. When I was at the most serious part of the crucifixion, a table of people close to the stage began to laugh. It was only through the grace of God that

I finished the drama.

Following the program, the lady in charge apologized. I was so upset. I could not wait to get out of there. When I got to my van I just draped myself across the steering wheel and said, "Oh God, I can't do this. They just made fun of your Son." And again, while I vented to the Lord (by the way He can take it), the Lord had enough of me and said, "Betty (He always uses my name), I never said it would be easy, I just asked you to remain faithful."

That night I dried my tears, and since then I have never looked back.

REFLECTIONS ON HEAVEN

"Death is swallowed up in victory." I Corinthians 15:54

The blind hymn writer, Fanny Crosby's soul song was the chorus of *Some Day the Silver Chord will Break.* She sang this song whenever she felt sorry for herself. If she got lost, got on the wrong train, or stumbled and fell, Fanny said, "I just stopped long enough to sing this song, cry, and then dry my tears and go on."

Remember she was blind, but she sang:

> And I shall see Him face to face
> And tell my story, saved by grace
> And I, (Fanny Jane) shall see Him face to face,
> And tell my story, saved by grace.

Fanny's quote: "It won't be long now, and I can hardly wait, His will be the first face that these eyes will ever behold, and I will be able to thank Him for saving me by His wonderful, marvelous grace."

I know it will not be long for me, and I too long to see Him face to face. I long to be reunited with those who have gone before me.

My Granny Martin used to long to go to heaven. She sang to me, an old hymn entitled *Eastern Gate.* She would sing, "I will meet you in the morning, just inside the Eastern Gate."

The year my mother passed away, Don Wyrtzen had just written the song *Finally Home.* That song has been a great comfort to me for many years.

The closer to 'home' I get, the more I sing the chorus of this song.

> And think of stepping on shore, and finding it heaven
> Of touching a hand, and finding it God's
> Of breathing new air, and finding it celestial
> Of waking up in Glory, and finding it Home.

Elvin and Betty Gray
Elvina and Love

Julesburg, Colorado
- 1965

Betty Gray and Love (Gray) Lockman

BONUS SECTION

FAVORITE VERSES

"You intended to harm me, but God intended it for good to accomplish what is now being done, the saving of many lives." Genesis 50:20 (NIV)

"For I know the plans I have for you," declares the Lord, "plans to prosper you and not to harm you, plans to give you hope and a future." Jeremiah 29:11 (NIV)

GRANNY MARTIN QUOTES

"People who don't like to go the church will sure be out of place in heaven."

"A clean Bible means a dirty life."

"This book will keep you from sin, or sin will keep you from this book."
Written in the front of Granny Martin's Bible

FAVORITE QUOTES

"A woman without the fragrance of Christ is like a silk flower."
Unknown

"God does not comfort us to make us comfortable, but to make us comforters."
Unknown

"God whispers to us in our pleasures, speaks in our conscience, but shouts to us in our pains; it is His megaphone to rouse a deaf world."
C. S. Lewis

"Our knees don't knock when we kneel on them."
Unknown

"If you never know me you will have missed nothing. But, if you never know my Lord, you will have missed everything."
Unknown

"He is no fool, to give what he cannot keep, to gain what he cannot lose."
Jim Eliot killed by Aucus Indians in Ecuador

"Don't be afraid of tomorrow, for God is already there."
Unknown

"Young at heart; other parts slightly older."
Unknown

"God, I don't understand you, but I do trust you."
Unknown

"The rooster may crow, but it is the hen that delivers."
Unknown

BETTY'S QUOTES FROM THE PLATFORM
WISPING *"Wallowing In Self Pity"*

"Be like the wise men of old, after they had been with Jesus, they went home a different way."

"Will you always try to remember that everyone you meet, sits by a pool of his or her own tears?"

"Tears are the sea-salt of the heart."

"Anger is just one letter away from danger."

In the movie "Dances with Wolves," the actor, Kevin Costner, is given the name "Dances with Wolves" by the Indians. If you were named for what you did, what would it be?

"God and prayer go together. To neglect one is to neglect the other."

You say, "My problem is too small to bother God." "My child, all problems are small to God."

"I can love God only as much as I love the person I dislike the most."

"God doesn't show us how bad we are, but how good we can become."

"A friend is a present you give yourself."

"God is never in a hurry, but He is never late."

"You can do what you please, when what you do pleases God."

FEAR knocked at my door, FAITH answered, and no one was there.

Sin
Sin takes us farther than we want to go.
Leaves a debt more than we can pay.
Keeps us longer than we want to stay.

Hey Diddle-Diddle
Hey diddle-diddle, I'm watching my middle,
I'm hoping to whittle it soon.
But eating's such fun, I won't get it done,
'Till my dish runs away with the spoon.

LOVE AND ELVINA'S
STORIES

THE OXYGEN TENT

Love Lockman

"We do not have a high priest who is unable to sympathize with our weaknesses, but we have one who has been tempted in every way, just as we are – yet was without sin. Let us then approach the throne of grace with confidence, so that we may receive mercy and find grace to help us in our time of need."
Hebrews 4:15-16 (NIV)

When our youngest and third son Stephen was just four months old, he awoke one morning with the worst cough I had ever heard. My husband Bill said, "That sounds like the croup to me."

The croup. I heard that word a lot while I was growing up whenever my sister or I woke us with a hoarse, raspy cough. I would overhear my mom talking on the phone to the doctor's office, "Yes, that's right. She has a fever, sore throat and a croupy cough." But to be quite honest, I never knew anyone who actually had the croup until many years later.

Stephen's cough that morning could be heard all over the house. If you've never heard a child with the croup, they sound like a goose honking or a seal barking with an almost metallic 'clank' at the end. And each time the cough came, Stephen's little four-month-old body would heave violently.

When I took Stephen to the doctor that day, the doctor informed me that the croup was a viral infection and would pretty much have to run its course. He gave me some medicines to help with the symptoms and sent me home with the warning, "Stephen will most likely get worse before he gets better, so don't panic during the night when he does. But by morning you should see some improvement."

It was a long night. Bill and I took turns walking the floor with Stephen because he wanted to be held. The doctor instructed us to take him into the bathroom and turn on the hot water in the shower and let him breath in the warm steam. And then we were to take him out into the cool night air immediately following. The contrast was supposed to help break up his congestion.

The doctor was right. Stephen did get much worse during the night. But he was also wrong. When morning came, Stephen wasn't getting better. When the doctor's office opened the next morning, I was sitting in the parking lot waiting. As soon as the doctor saw Stephen's condition, he immediately sent us to the local hospital where Stephen was admitted to pediatric intensive care. I called Bill and told him where we were. As soon as he got the two older boys off to school, he met me at the hospital.

As they were getting Stephen's room ready, they brought in a metal frame baby bed with a plastic oxygen tent set up over the entire crib. Bill convinced me that this would be a good time to go home and pack a few things and come back because he knew I would want to be by Stephen's bedside until he was released. I quickly and reluctantly headed for home while Bill stayed and rocked Stephen.

While I was gone the nurse came in and instructed Bill to put Stephen in the oxygen tent. She said, "A mist mixed with medicines to break up his congestion and make him breathe easier is vaporized from the top of that tent. The mist will permeate his entire environment, and slowly he will begin to get better. But these next few hours are crucial. You can reach in through that zippered slot in the plastic and pat him. But he's pretty much in his own little world in there."

There was only one problem. When Bill tried to lay Stephen down inside the oxygen tent, he became frantic and began crying. The crying made his congestion even worse so Bill would pick him up again. After all, everybody knows that a sick baby wants to be held.

But when the nurse came back in and saw Stephen in Bill's arms and not in the oxygen tent she sternly said, "Mr. Lockman, that baby has got to go inside that tent now!" Bill tried to explain the dilemma of putting Stephen down and his crying making things worse, but the nurse wasn't buying the story. "Doctor's orders are that baby has got to be inside that tent," she barked, "so when I come back he had better be in there or you'll have to leave."

When I returned to the hospital room, I saw a very strange, and yet a very moving sight. I saw my six-foot-tall husband all curled up on this tiny baby bed inside the oxygen tent holding Stephen in his arms. Bill's back was to me so he didn't see me enter the room. The mist was spraying in his face as he rocked Stephen back and forth so he didn't hear me either. But I heard him. And I'll never forget what he was saying to our son.

As he held Stephen close to his chest, he kept saying over and over, "It's gonna be okay, Stevie. You're safe in Daddy's arms. And I love you." Again and again I heard the same message as I stood and watched with tears streaming, "It's gonna be okay, Stevie. You're safe in Daddy's arms. And I love you."

As I stood there and watched this scene unfold, it dawned on me that this is exactly what God did for me. He didn't sit in heaven and say, "Boy, I wish there was some way I could help Love, some way I could relate to her." No, instead He cared so much for me that He came into 'my own little world' to hold me in the hard times.

The book of Hebrews says that we have a High Priest who has gone through everything that we will ever face just so He can relate to us. Do you know how much God loves you? I don't think any of us really have a clue. Can I be honest? If you were drowning, I'd do everything within my power to save you. But if one of my boys were drowning at the same time, you better hope you can tread water. Until my son is out of the water, I'm sorry but you're on your own. This is nothing personal, just a parent's love.

But our Heavenly Father chose us when His only Son was drowning. When Jesus was drowning in our sins on a cross, God chose messed-up me and messed-up you. That is love undefinable, at least from our standpoint!

When I'm hurting, when I'm sick, when I'm afraid or find myself alone in a strange place, I feel the Father's arms around me and I hear His loving voice say, "It's going to be okay, Love. You're safe in your Daddy's arms. And I love you."

If you are a child of God, there is nothing that will ever happen to you that didn't first pass through a nail-scarred hand before it got to you. And

He will use the worst thing that could possibly happen to you to prove His unconditional love for you.

And oh yeah, by the way, it's going to be okay. You're safe in your Daddy's arms. And He loves you.

"God demonstrates his own love for us in this: While we were still sinners, Christ died for us." Romans 5:8

Footnote: Whatever you are going through, your Heavenly Father climbs into your little world and holds you in His arms and says, "It is going to be all right, for you are safe in your Daddy's arms and I love you"

When Julie Nevel heard me tell this story, she wrote this song ...In Daddy's Arms.

In Daddy's Arms
The hours passed and their baby's cough was getting worse;
As his mom and dad did all the doctors told them first.
Finally they rushed him to intensive care;
A tent for oxygen, they'd have to leave him there.

Ev'ry time his daddy laid him down, the more he'd cry, the worse he'd sound;
So he'd pick him up to comfort him again.
A few more tries with no success, the baby clearly in distress;
The nurse said, "Sir, he must go in the tent to breathe;
If you can't put him down you'll have to leave."
The mother walked the halls and prayed a desperate prayer;
When she went back in the room, this is what she saw there.
Her husband by their baby's side, this grown man all curled up inside;
Holding close their precious one, repeating these words to his son.

Chorus
It's gonna be ok, it's gonna be alright;
You're safe in your daddy's arms tonight.
You gotta know your daddy loves you and believe he's here to stay;
It's gonna be alright, it's gonna be ok.

Lately does it seem like life is closing in;
You can hardly breathe, feel like you can't win.
Angry thoughts are tearing you apart inside;
You just want to run, but there's no place to hide

God creator of it all put on flesh and became small;
Wrapped His loving arms around the life He gave to you.
He will not leave your side, He'll see you through.

Chorus
It's gonna be ok, it's gonna be alright;
You're safe in your Daddy's arms tonight.
You gotta know your Daddy loves you and believe He's here to stay;
It's gonna be alright, it's gonna be ok.

Words & Music by Julie Nevel, 2004 Nevel Music (Used by permission)

LEFT IN GOOD HANDS

Elvina McEwen

From the day that you welcome them into the world you begin to prepare to say goodbye.

It was the day I'd dreaded since my oldest son Michael was accepted into a college two hours away from home. He looked upon his move to a new apartment as an adventure. I looked upon it with dread. Dreams of what he was going to accomplish and experience occupied our conversations for weeks. I was determined not to spoil his joy and anticipation with a flood of tears.

Michael was comfortably settled into his new apartment. Boxes and suitcases had all been unpacked. His refrigerator and pantry were fully stocked. It was time for his father, younger brother, and me to say goodbye. I excused myself to the small bathroom to have a pep talk with myself in the mirror. Who was this woman staring back at me in the mirror? Shouldn't she be holding a blond toddler instead of walking away from a young man who towered over her?

The pep talk worked wonders until Michael walked us to the car and kissed me on the top of my head. Our good byes were quick, with promises that he'd call us the next day. I patted myself on the back for holding the tears until I turned to walk away. The tears opened like a floodgate when I closed the car door. Our drive home was almost in complete silence as I had flashbacks of Michael's childhood.

I had only one prayer on my lips on the drive home and for the rest of the weekend, "Please God, take care of my son! Please give me a sign that he will be all right. Please send your angels to protect him."

The rest of the weekend went by at a snail's pace. There had been telephone calls from Michael assuring me that he was doing great. I sat through the Sunday morning church service hanging on every word of the songs and sermon, fully expecting to receive a sign. I prayed and waited quietly, expectantly. But no sign came.

Sign or no sign I would have to trust that Michael was going to be okay.

Teaching second grade leaves little time during the day to think about personal problems. My focus was on the new school year and the week that was ahead of me when a mother of one of my students from last year stopped me in the hall. "Mrs. McEwen, Matthew likes his new teacher, but says that it's not the same as being in your room. I asked him to tell me what he missed most, and he said it was the angels in your classroom."

My room is a colorful jumble of seasonal decorations and educational displays. I teach in a Christian school, but I'd never displayed angels. Matthew's mother continued, "I asked him to explain about the angels. He said that there were always three angels who were in your classroom. One who stood at the door and two who moved about the children. He said they never spoke but he'd smiled at them and they'd smiled back at him. Matthew said he always felt safe in your room because they were there." She went on to described how he'd gone into great detail about how they looked.

The poor mother must have thought I was having a nervous breakdown. I began to cry, gave her a quick hug, and told her I'd have to explain later, but she had been an answer to my prayer.

Since my boys were babies, I've prayed that the angels of the Lord would encamp around them to keep them safe. I'd thanked God on many occasions when I knew that it could have only been angels that had kept them from harm. Why would I doubt that angels would not follow Michael to college? Relief flooded over me and tears puddled on my desk. I'd been looking for a sign, and I received it where I least expected, in the hallway of my own school.

I tried with all my might to see the angels in my classroom, but no vision appeared. Yet the thought that the children in my classroom had angels ministering to them was a comfort to know that Michael had his own angels two hours away.

I shared Matthew's story of the angels with my husband and a close friend. It was too priceless to risk hearing comments of how cute it was or to have someone marvel over a child's imagination.

Weeks went by and although Michael wasn't homesick, I was homesick for him. His empty chair at the dinner table seemed to mock me. I found myself waking in the middle of the night thinking I hadn't heard the back-door close before curfew. His empty bedroom was a reflection of a room in my heart. I wondered if this empty feeling would ever fully go away?

My answer came again at school. During art class the children had been told they could use their new colored pencils to draw whatever they wished. Lexi spent her free time after the lesson to finish up her masterpiece. With great pride she brought her picture to me as a gift. Before she could explain her artwork, tears welled up in my eyes. There was no explanation necessary. Looking back at me on the paper were three angels, dressed in the colors Matthew had described to his mother.

Lexi's artwork is lovingly displayed over my desk. It only takes a glance at the picture to be reminded that I can trust that Michael is in good hands.

Saying goodbye is never easy. But knowing that those you love are in even better hands than your own is reassuring.

OPEN DOORS FOR MINISTRY

"How beautiful are the feet of those who bring good news! Romans 10:15b (NIV)

These are just a few of the many doors God has opened up for Betty.

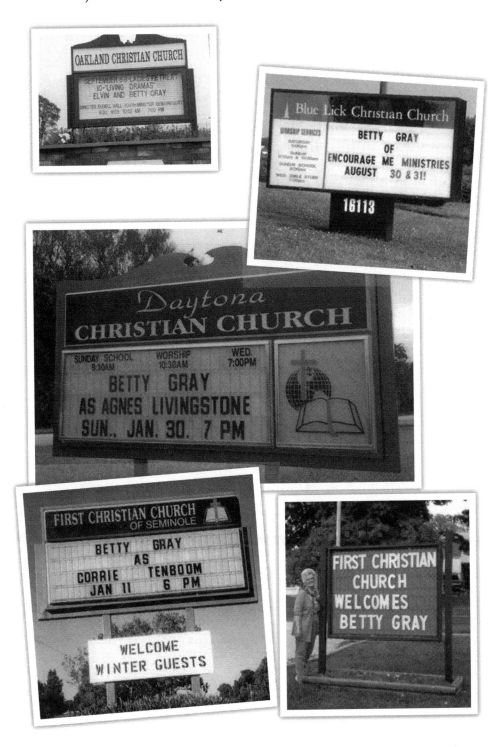

National Story Telling 2004, Jonesville, Tennessee

Bicentennial Musical Celebration
July 4, 1976
Jackson Co., Indiana

87828147R00086

Made in the USA
Lexington, KY
01 May 2018